Ada Quality and S

Guidelines for Professional Programmers

The Software Productivity Consortium

Ada Quality and Style
Guidelines for Professional Programmers

The Software Productivity Consortium

VNR VAN NOSTRAND REINHOLD
New York

Printed in the United States of America

Van Nostrand Reinhold
115 Fifth Avenue
New York, New York 10003

Van Nostrand Reinhold International Company Limited
11 New Fetter Lane
London EC4P 4EE, England

Van Nostrand Reinhold
480 La Trobe Street
Melbourne, Victoria 3000, Australia

Nelson Canada
1120 Birchmount Road
Scarborough, Ontario M1K 5G4, Canada

16   15   14   13   12   11   10   9   8   7   6   5   4   3   2   1

Library of Congress Cataloging-in-Publication Data

ADA quality and style: guidelines for professional programmers/
  Software Productivity Consortium.
       p. cm
   Includes index.
   ISBN 0-442-23805-3
   1. ADA (Computer program language) I. Software Productivity
Consortium.
QA76.73.A35A335 1989   89-8968
005.13'3--dc20

AUTHORS AND ACKNOWLEDGEMENTS

Production of this book has been very much a team effort. Samuel Gregory, Margaret Skalko, Lyn Uzzle and Richard Drake wrote most of the original material. They are Software Productivity Consortium Members of Technical Staff with over 20 years of Ada programming experience between them. Paul Cohen, as leader of the Software Productivity Consortium Ada Project, initiated the work, and guided it through its early stages. Robert Mathis (consultant) contributed material on Ada numerics and provided substantial support and criticism.

Henry Ledgard led an intensive review of the first draft, providing invaluable advice on the book's structure and content. The final editing process was mainly conducted by Samuel Gregory. It was coordinated by John Knight, who with Mark Dowson, wrote the introductory sections.

Special thanks are due to Debra Morgan, whose efficiency and patience while retyping innumerable drafts made production of the book possible.

Numerous other staff of the Software Productivity Consortium, and several outside consultants, contributed review, comment and support. They include:

Bruce Barnes
Alex Blakemore
Terry Bollinger
Charles Brown
Neil Burkhard
William Carlson
Susan Carroll
John Chludzinski
Vicki Clatterbuck
Robert Cohen
Elizabeth Comer
Daniel Cooper
Jorge Diaz–Herrera
   (George Mason University)
Timothy Harrison
Robert Hofkin

Allan Jaworski
Edward Jones
John A.N. Lee
   (Virginia Tech)
Eric Marshall
Charles Mooney
John Moore
Karl Nyberg (consultant)
Arthur Pyster
Samuel Redwine, Jr.
William Riddle
Lisa Smith
Frederick Stluka
Kathy Velick
David Weiss
Howard Yudkin

VAX™ is a trademark of Digital Equipment Corp.

Contents

Chapter 1

Introduction

This book is intended to help the computer professional produce better Ada programs. It presents a set of specific guidelines for using the powerful features of Ada in a disciplined manner. Each guideline consists of a concise statement of the principles that should be followed, and a rationale explaining why following the guideline is important. In most cases, an example of the use of the guideline is provided, and in some cases a further example is included showing the consequences of violating the guideline. Possible exceptions to the application of the guideline are explicitly noted, and further explanatory notes included where appropriate. Many of the guidelines are specific enough to be adopted as corporate or project programming standards. Others require a managerial decision on a particular instantiation before they can be used as standards. These issues are discussed in Section 1.4 of this introduction. Other sections of the introduction discuss how this book should be used by various categories of software development personnel.

Ada was designed to support the development of high quality, reliable, reusable, portable software. For a number of reasons, no programming language can ensure the achievement of these desirable objectives on its own. For example, programming must be embedded in a disciplined development process that addresses requirements analysis, design, implementation, verification, validation and maintenance in an organized and well managed way. The use of the language must conform to good programming practices based on well established software engineering principles. This book is intended to help bridge the gap between these principles and the actual practice of programming in Ada.

Clear, readable, understandable source text eases program evolution, adaptation, and maintenance. First, such source text is more likely to be correct and reliable. Second, effective code adaptation is a prerequisite to code reuse, a technique that has the potential for drastic reductions in system development cost. Easy adaptation requires a thorough understanding of the software, and that is facilitated considerably by clarity. Finally, since maintenance (really evolution) is a costly process that continues throughout the life of a system, clarity plays a major role in keeping maintenance costs down. Over the entire life cycle, code has to be read and understood far more often than it is written; the investment of effort in writing readable, understandable code is thus well worthwhile. Many of the guidelines in this book are designed to promote clarity of the source text.

There are two main aspects of code clarity. Careful and consistent layout of the source text on the page or the screen can enhance readability dramatically. Similarly, careful attention to the structure of code can make it easier to understand. This is true both on the small scale, for example by judicious choice of identifier names or by disciplined use of loops, and on the large scale, for example by proper use of packages. Both layout and structure are treated by these guidelines.

Commentary in source text is a contentious issue. There are arguments both for and against the view that comments enhance readability. The biggest problem with comments in practice is that people often fail to update them when the associated source text is changed, thereby making the commentary misleading. We take the position that commentary should be minimized, and largely reserved for highlighting cases where there are overriding reasons to violate one of the guidelines. As far as possible, source text should use self-explanatory names for objects and program units, and use simple, understandable, program structures so that little if any additional commentary is needed. The extra effort in selecting (and entering) appropriate names, and the extra thought needed to design clean and understandable program structures are fully justified.

Programming texts often fail to discuss overall program structure; we include a chapter addressing it. The majority of the guidelines in that chapter are concerned with the application of sound software engineering principles such as information hiding and separation of concerns. The chapter is neither a textbook on nor an introduction to these principles; rather it indicates how they can be realized using the features of Ada.

A number of other guidelines are particularly concerned with reliability and portability issues. They counsel avoidance of language features and programming practices that either depend on properties not defined in Ada or on properties that may vary from implementation to implementation. Some of these guidelines, such as the one forbidding dependence on expression evaluation order, should never be violated. Others may have to be violated in special situations such as interfacing to other systems. This should only be done after careful deliberation, and such violations should be prominently indicated. Performance constraints are often offered as an excuse for unsafe programming practices; this is very rarely a sufficient justification.

Software tools could be used to enforce, encourage, or check conformance to many of the guidelines. At present, few such tools are available for Ada beyond code formatters or syntax directed editors. Existing code formatters are often parameterizable, and can be instantiated to lay out code in a way consistent with the guidelines in this book.

This book is intended for those involved in the development of real software systems written in Ada. Below, we discuss how they can make the most effective use of the material presented. Readers with different levels of Ada experience and different roles in a software project will need to exploit the book in different ways; we address specific comments to three broad categories of software development personnel: those new to Ada, experienced Ada programmers, and software development managers.

1.1 HOW TO USE THIS BOOK

There are a number of ways in which this book can be used: as a reference on good Ada style; as a comprehensive list of guidelines which, if followed, will result in better Ada programs; or as a reference work to consult about the use of specific features of the language. The book contains many guidelines, some of which are quite complex. Learning them all at the same time should not be necessary; it is unlikely that you will be using all the features of the language at once, so you will not need to keep all the guidelines in mind at one time. However, we recommend that all programmers (and, where possible, other Ada project staff) make an effort to read and understand Chapters 2, 3, 4 and Chapter 5 up to Section 5.7. Some of the material is quite difficult (for example, Section 4.2 which discusses visibility) but it covers issues which are fundamental to the effective use of Ada, and is important for any software professional involved in building Ada systems.

The remainder of the book covers relatively specific issues: Exceptions and Erroneous Execution at the end of Chapter 5, and Tasking, Portability and Reuse in Chapters 6, 7 and 8 respectively. You should be aware of the content of this part of the book, and may be required to follow the guidelines presented in it, but you could defer more detailed study until the need arises. Meanwhile, it can serve as useful reference material about specific Ada features, for example the discussion of floating point numbers in the chapter on portability.

Chapter 9 is directed at software project managers. It lists those guidelines that need to be instantiated to be used as standards, and indicates the instantiation that has been adopted in the guidelines' examples. Chapter 10 consists of an extended example of an Ada program that conforms to the guidelines presented.

This book is not intended as an introductory text on Ada or as a complete manual of the Ada language. If you are learning Ada you should equip yourself with a good introduction to the language such as Barnes [4] or Cohen [8]. The Ada Language Reference Manual [28] (Ada LRM) should be regarded as a crucial companion volume to this book. The majority of guidelines reference the sections of the Ada LRM that define the language features being discussed. Appendix A cross references sections of the Ada LRM to the guidelines.

Throughout the book, references are given to other sources of information about Ada style and other Ada issues. The works referenced are listed at the end of the book, followed by a bibliography which includes them and other relevant sources consulted during the book's preparation.

1.2   TO THE NEW Ada PROGRAMMER

At first sight, Ada offers a bewildering variety of features; Ada is a powerful tool intended to solve difficult problems and almost every feature has a legitimate application in some context. This makes it especially important to use Ada's features in a disciplined and organized way. The guidelines in this book forbid the use of few Ada features. Rather, they show how the features can be systematically deployed to write clear, high quality programs. Following the guidelines will make learning Ada easier and help you to master its apparent complexity. From the very beginning, you will be writing programs that exploit the best features of the language in the way that the designers intended.

Programmers experienced in using another programming language are often tempted to use Ada as if it were their familiar language, but with irritating syntactic differences. This pitfall should be avoided at all costs; it can lead to convoluted code that subverts exactly those aspects of Ada that make it so suitable for building high quality systems. You must learn to "think Ada"; following the guidelines in this book and reading the examples of their use will help you to do this as quickly and painlessly as possible.

To some degree, novice programmers learning Ada have an advantage. Following the guidelines from the very beginning will help in developing a clear programming style that effectively exploits the language. If you are in this category, we recommend that you adopt the guidelines even for those exercises you perform as part of learning Ada. Initially, developing sound programming habits by concentrating on the guidelines themselves, and their supporting examples, is more important than understanding the rationale for each guideline. Note that each chapter ends with a summary of the guidelines it contains.

1.3   TO THE EXPERIENCED Ada PROGRAMMER

As an experienced programmer you will already be writing code that conforms to many of the guidelines in this book. In some areas, however, you may have adopted a personal programming style that differs from that presented here, and you might be reluctant to change. We strongly recommend that you carefully review those guidelines that are inconsistent with your current style, make sure that you understand their rationale, and consider adopting them. The overall set of guidelines in this book embodies a consistent and proven approach to producing high quality programs which would be weakened by too many exceptions.

Another important reason for general adoption of common guidelines is consistency. If all the staff of a project write source text in the same style, many critical project activities will be easier. Consistent code simplifies formal and informal code reviews, system integration, within–project code reuse and the provision and application of supporting tools. In practice, corporate or project standards may require any deviations from the guidelines to be explicitly commented, so adopting a non–standard approach may involve you in extra work.

1.4   TO THE SOFTWARE PROJECT MANAGER

Technical management has a key role to play in ensuring that the software produced in the course of a project is correct, reliable, maintainable, and portable. Management must create a project–wide commitment to the production of high–quality code; define project–specific coding standards and guidelines; foster an understanding of why uniform adherence to the chosen coding standards is critical to product quality; and establish policies and procedures to check and enforce that adherence. The guidelines contained in this book can aid such an effort.

An important activity for managers is the definition of coding standards for a project or organization. These guidelines do not, in themselves, constitute a complete set of standards, but can serve as a basis for them. A number of guidelines advise that consistent decisions be taken about some aspect of source text, indicate a reasonable range of decisions, but do not prescribe a particular decision. For example, the second guideline in the book (Guideline 2.1.2) advocates using a consistent number of spaces for indentation, and indicates in the rationale that 2 – 4 spaces would be reasonable. With your senior technical staff, you should review each such guideline and arrive at a decision about its instantiation (in the example above, perhaps 3 spaces) that will constitute your project or organizational standard. To support this process, Chapter 9 of the book lists all guidelines that need instantiation to be used as standards. It also gives a possible instantiation for each guideline that corresponds to the decision adopted by the authors of this book, and used in the extended example of Chapter 10. In addition, the guidelines requiring instantiation are marked in the earlier chapters with a double dagger (‡).

Two other areas require managerial decisions about standardization. Guideline 3.1.4 advises avoidance of arbitrary abbreviations as or as part of object or unit names. You should prepare a glossary of acceptable abbreviations for a project that allows the use of shorter versions of application specific terms (e.g. FFT for Fast Fourier Transform or SPN for Stochastic Petri Net). You should try to keep this glossary short, and restrict it to terms which will need to be frequently used as part of names; having to continually refer to an extensive glossary to understand source text makes it hard to read.

The portability guidelines given in Chapter 7 need careful attention. We strongly advise that you insist on adherence to them even if the need to port the resulting software is not currently foreseen. Following the guidelines will improve the potential reusability of the resulting code in projects which use different Ada implementations. At the very least, you should insist that where particular project exigencies force the relaxation of some of the portability guidelines, non–portable features of the source text are prominently indicated. Observing the Chapter 7 guidelines will require definition and standardization of project or organization specific numeric types to use in place of the (potentially non–portable) predefined numeric types.

Your decisions on the above standardization issues should be incorporated in a project or organization coding standards document. If you do not deviate too far from the guidelines in this book, that document will be quite short (two or three pages), which improves its chance of being read and followed by project staff. Of course, you will have to provide sufficient copies of the book, particularly for new or junior project staff, to ensure their ready access to the guidelines.

With coding standards in place, you need to ensure adherence to them. Probably the most important aspect of this is gaining the wholehearted commitment of your senior programming staff to their use. Given this commitment, and the example of high quality Ada being produced by your best programmers, it will be far easier to conduct effective formal code reviews that check compliance to project standards.

Consistent coding standards also simplify the cost–effective provision of automated tools to support your programmers and to check the quality of their product. If you have a tools group in your project or organization, they can be tasked to acquire or develop tools to support your standards. If not, you at least have a systematic basis for evaluating programming tools for acquisition or development.

Some general issues concerning the management of Ada projects are discussed by Foreman and Goodenough [11].

Chapter 2

Source Code Presentation

The physical layout of source text on the page or screen has a strong influence on its readability. This chapter includes simple guidelines that, if followed, will ease the task of the reader.

The issue of formatting Ada source code has been treated in many existing style guides and programming standards documents. The rationale for such treatment is the readability requirement, in Section 1.3 of the Ada LRM [28]. It is important for the code to be well structured in terms of indentation and naming standards; however, the definition of good structure is often subjective.

A number of the guidelines define general principles of good layout, but do not prescribe a particular layout style. The decisions on exactly how to instantiate these principles are better left to the responsible party in a project or organization.

Entirely consistent layout is hard to achieve or check manually, and, if possible should be automated with a tool for parameterized code formatting or the guidelines incorporated into an automatic coding template. The resulting presentation of the code will then be consistent to the human reader, and conform to the documentation conventions determined by program management.

2.1 CODE FORMATTING

The "code formatting" of Ada source code affects how the code looks, not what the code does. Topics included here are horizontal spacing, indentation, alignment, pagination, and line length. The most important guideline is to be consistent throughout the compilation unit as well as the project. To enhance reusability, do not make a style choice that precludes reformatting.

7

2.1.1   Horizontal Spacing ‡

guideline

- Employ a consistent spacing strategy around delimiters.

example

The following is the sample instantiation of this guideline given in Chapter 10. It is used throughout the examples.

- Employ at least one blank before and after the following delimiters: & * + / : < = > | => .. := /= >= <= << >> <> and - used as a binary operator.

- Precede the minus sign used as a unary operator by at least one blank.

- Do not leave spaces before or after ′ . ** unless involved in a line break.

- Except when in conflict with other parts of this instantiation, leave at least one blank on the non-literal side of ′ and " when they delimit a character and a string literal, respectively.

- Do not leave spaces before or after parentheses which delimit argument lists or array indices.

- Where parentheses delimit an expression, leave at least one blank before the left parenthesis and after the right parenthesis, but not between multiple left or multiple right parentheses.

- Leave one blank before and after a short (1 character) identifier or literal within parentheses.

- Leave at least one blank after but no space before ; and , even if they follow a right parenthesis.

These spacing standards produce the following code fragments:

```
REGISTER(PC) := REGISTER( A );

OPERATOR_PRECEDENCE_MNEMONICS : STRING := "My Dog Ain't Smart,"
                              & " but he obeys"
                              & " My Dear Aunt Sallie.";

ARRAY_NAME(INDEX) := MEMORY(ARRAY_BASE_ADDRESS + (INDEX * ELEMENT_LENGTH));

GET_NEXT_VALUE(SENSOR);

type SIGNED_WHOLE_16 is range -(2**15) .. (2**15) - 1;
```

rationale

Spacing enhances readability since the white space emphasizes delimiters on a source statement line. Consistent spacing aids visual recognition of constructs irrespective of where they occur in program text.

The use of the ampersand and layout of the partial strings in the example above is as intended by the language designers. It clarifies what is going on and allows construction of string literals longer than the line length. In natural language usage, the colon is flush with what precedes it. In Ada, it is a tabulator, or a column separator (see Guideline 2.1.4).

note

The example instantiation of the guidelines specifies <u>minimum</u> spacings around delimiters in various circumstances. Subject to these restrictions, the <u>actual</u> spacings will be determined by the need for vertical alignment (See Guidelines 2.1.3, 2.1.4, 2.1.5).

A code formatter can enforce these spacing standards or change code to meet them as needed. Your organization's standards or personal preferences may be different from the conventions stated above. If you are charged with setting the standards, recognize that others' satisfaction and sense of aesthetics may ultimately be more important to a successful project than your own.

2.1.2 Indentation ‡

guideline

- Indent and align nested control structures, continuation lines, and embedded units consistently.

- Distinguish between indentation for statement–list structure and for continuation lines.

- Use a series of spaces for indentation, not the tab character ([18] §2.2).

example

```
begin -- EXAMPLE

  loop

    TIO.DISPLAY_MENU("Example Menu", EXAMPLE_MENU, USER_CHOICE);

    case USER_CHOICE is
      when 'A'   =>
        ITEM := TIO.GET("Item to add");
      when 'D'   =>
        ITEM := TIO.GET("Item to delete");
      when 'M'   =>
        ITEM := TIO.GET("Item to modify");
      when 'Q'   =>
        exit;
      when others =>
        null;        -- already caught by TIO.DISPLAY_MENU
    end case;

  end loop;

end EXAMPLE;
```

rationale

Indentation improves the readability of the code because it allows a reader to "see" the structure of a program. The levels of modularity are clearly identified by indentation and the first and last keywords in a construct can be matched visually.

While there is much discussion on the number of spaces to indent, the reason for indentation is code clarity. According to Schneiderman ([23] page 7), "A modest level of indentation (2–4 spaces) has been shown to be beneficial." The fact that the code is indented consistently is more important than the number of spaces used for indentation. If a configurable editor is not available, and a change is desired, a code formatter can be obtained to do the job.

Additionally, the Ada LRM ([28] §1.5) contains recommended paragraphing. "Different lines are used for parts of a syntax rule if the corresponding parts of the construct described by the rule are intended to be on different lines." It also states that "... all indentation be multiples of a basic step of indentation (the number of spaces for the basic step is not defined)."

Use of spaces rather than the tab character for indentation enhances portability because the treatment of tab characters is a function of a terminal or printer parameter setting.

Some systems permit the use of the tab key but physically insert the appropriate number of spaces. In such cases the use of the tab key does not imply the use of tabs. In any other circumstance, it is very difficult to get tabs right.

note

According to Ada LRM ([28] §1.5) , "... On the other hand, if a complete construct can fit on one line, this is allowed in the recommended paragraphing." If the code is getting close to the right hand margin, it would be prudent to modify this guideline on a local basis as long as such modifications are consistent, well marked, and the guideline practice is restored immediately afterward. See Guideline 2.1.8.

2.1.3   Alignment of Operators

guideline

- Align operators vertically to emphasize local program structure.

example

```
if SLOT_A >= SLOT_B then
   TEMPORARY := SLOT_A;
   SLOT_A    := SLOT_B;
   SLOT_B    := TEMPORARY;
end if;

NUMERATOR    := (B**2) - (4 * A * C);
DENOMINATOR := 2 * A;
SOLUTION_1   := -B + SQUARE_ROOT(NUMERATOR / DENOMINATOR);
SOLUTION_2   :=  B + SQUARE_ROOT(NUMERATOR / DENOMINATOR);

X :=    A * B
      + C * D
      + E * F;

Y := (A * B) + C      -- basic equation
      - 3.5           -- error factor
      + (2 * D) - E    -- account for ...
```

rationale

Alignment makes it easier to see the position of the operators and, therefore, puts visual emphasis on what the code is doing.

The use of lines and spacing on long expressions can emphasize terms, precedence of operators, and other semantics. It can also leave room for highlighting comments within an expression.

exceptions

If vertical alignment of operators forces a statement to be broken over two lines, and especially if the break is at an inappropriate spot, it may be preferable to relax the alignment guideline.

2.1.4   Alignment of Declarations

guideline

- Organize declarations as a table.

- Provide at most one declaration per line (see also Guideline 2.1.8).

example

Declarations of enumeration literals can be tabularized:

```
type OP_CODES is (
    PUSH,                   POP,
    ADD,                    SUBTRACT,
    MULTIPLY,               DIVIDE,
    ...
    SUBROUTINE_CALL,        SUBROUTINE_RETURN
    BRANCH,                 BRANCH_ON_ZERO,
    BRANCH_ON_NEGATIVE,     BLOCK_MOVE
    );
```

Variable and constant declarations can be in columns separated by the symbols :
:= and --

```
PROMPT_COLUMN : constant          := 40;
QUESTION_MARK : constant STRING := " ? ";   -- prompt on error input
PROMPT_STRING : constant STRING := " ==> ";
```

or with each part on a separate line with its unique indentation level.

```
INPUT_LINE_BUFFER
    : USER_RESPONSE_TEXT_FRAME
        := (others => ' ');
            -- If the declaration needed a comment, it would fit here.
```

rationale

Many programming standards documents require tabular repetition of names, types, initial values, and meaning in unit header comments. These comments are redundant and can become inconsistent with the code. Aligning the declarations themselves in tabular fashion (see the examples) provides identical information to both compiler and reader, enforces at most one declaration per line, and eases maintenance by providing space for initializations and necessary comments. A tabular layout enhances readability, preventing names from "hiding" in a mass of declarations. In addition, the all-on-one-line style encourages the use of short full names. This applies to type declarations as well as object declarations.

2.1.5   More on Alignment ‡

guideline

- Align parameter modes and grouping symbols vertically.

- Use four trailing blanks for mode in and three leading blanks for mode out.

example

```
procedure DISPLAY_MENU (TITLE   : in    STRING;
                        OPTIONS : in    MENUS;
                        CHOICE  :   out ALPHA_NUMERICS);
```

or

```
procedure DISPLAY_MENU_ON_PRIMARY_WINDOW
  (TITLE   : in    STRING;
   OPTIONS : in    MENUS;
   CHOICE  :   out ALPHA_NUMERICS);
```

or

```
procedure DISPLAY_MENU (
  TITLE   : in    STRING;
  OPTIONS : in    MENUS;
  CHOICE  :   out ALPHA_NUMERICS
  );
```

Grouping symbol alignment makes complicated relational expressions more clear:

```
if (FIRST_CHARACTER not in ALPHA_NUMERICS) or else
   (not VALID_OPTION(FIRST_CHARACTER)    )          then
```

rationale

This facilitates readability and understandability. Aligning parameter modes provides the effect of a table with columns for parameter name, mode, type, and if necessary, parameter-specific comments. Vertical alignment of parameters across subprograms within a compilation unit increases the readability even more.

note

Various options are available for subprogram layout. The second example aligns the start of all subprogram names and all parameter names in a program, but has the disadvantage of occupying an unnecessary line where subprogram names are short, and looking awkward if there is only one parameter.

The third example has the advantage that one can add, delete, or reorder the parameter lines with little worry about the parentheses.

The last example shows alignment of a multiple condition if statement. The alignment emphasizes the variables that are tested and their relationships. The "or else" is by itself so the major connective operator is not lost in the expression. This helps the reader to parse it.

exceptions

If there is only one parameter, or if the same mode is used throughout the compilation unit, the extra blanks around modes may be omitted.

2.1.6   Blank Lines

guideline

- Use blank lines to group logically related lines of text [17].

example

```
if ... then

    for ... loop
        ...
    end loop;

end if;
```

This example separates different kinds of declarations with blank lines:

```
type EMPLOYEE_RECORD is
    record
        NAME          : NAME_STRING;
        DATE_OF_BIRTH : DATE;
        DATE_OF_HIRE  : DATE;
        SALARY        : MONEY;
    end record;

type DAY is (
    MONDAY,       TUESDAY,
    WEDNESDAY,    THURSDAY,
    FRIDAY,       SATURDAY,
    SUNDAY
    );

subtype WEEKDAY is DAY range MONDAY   .. FRIDAY;
subtype WEEKEND is DAY range SATURDAY .. SUNDAY;
```

rationale

When blank lines are used in a thoughtful and consistent manner, sections of related code are more visible to readers. Blank lines can be used to show modular organization, which has itself been shown to be useful ([23] page 7).

2.1.7   Pagination ‡

guideline

- Mark the top of the body of each program unit and the beginning and end of its frame.

- Mark the top and bottom of a package specification.

example

```
-----------------------------------------------------------------------
package body SPC_NUMERIC_TYPES is
   ...
-----------------------------------------------------------------------
   function MIN (LEFT  : in TINY_INTEGER;
                 RIGHT : in TINY_INTEGER)
      return TINY_INTEGER is

   begin
      if (LEFT > RIGHT) then
         return LEFT;
      else
         return RIGHT;
      end if;
   end MIN;
-----------------------------------------------------------------------
end SPC_NUMERIC_TYPES;
-----------------------------------------------------------------------
```

rationale

It is easy to overlook parts of program units that are not visible on the current page or screen. The page lengths of presentation hardware and software vary widely. By clearly marking the program's logical page boundaries, for example with a "dotted line," you enable a reader to check quickly whether all of a program unit is visible.

note

This guideline does not address code layout on the physical "page" because the dimensions of such pages vary widely and no single guideline is appropriate.

The frame of a program unit is delineated by the begin and end of its body. (Ada LRM [28] §11.2).

exception

If the visual distance between the beginning of a program unit and the beginning of its frame is small, the beginning-of-frame marker may be omitted.

2.1.8   Number of Statements per Line

guideline

- Start each statement on a new line.
- Write no more than one simple statement per line.
- Break compound statements over multiple lines.

example

```
-- Use
if END_OF_FILE then
   CLOSE_FILE;
else
   GET_NEXT_RECORD;
end if;

-- rather than
if END_OF_FILE then CLOSE_FILE; else GET_NEXT_RECORD; end if;

-- exceptional case
PUT("A="); PUT( A ); NEWLINE;
PUT("B="); PUT( B ); NEWLINE;
PUT("C="); PUT( C ); NEWLINE;
```

rationale

A single statement on each line enhances the reader's ability to find statements and helps prevent statements being missed. Similarly, the structure of a compound statement is clearer when its parts are on separate lines.

note

A source statement is any Ada language statement that is terminated with a semicolon. If the statement is longer than the remaining space on the line, continue it on the next line. This guideline includes declarations, context clauses, and subprogram parameters.

According to the Ada LRM, "The preferred places for other line breaks are after semicolons" ([28] §1.5).

exceptions

The example of PUT and NEWLINE statements shows a legitimate exception. This grouping of closely related statements on the same line makes the structural relationship between the groups clear.

2.1.9   Source Code Line Length ‡

guideline

•   Adhere to a maximum line length limit for source code ([18] §2.3).

rationale

When Ada code is ported from one system to another, there may be restrictions on the record size of source line statements, possibly for one of the following reasons: Some operating systems may not support variable length records for tape i/o; some operating systems reserve columns 73 and beyond for internal processing; some terminals support an 80-character line width with no line-wrap.

Source code must sometimes be published for various reasons, and letter–size paper is not as forgiving as a computer listing in terms of the number of usable columns.

There are also human limitations in the width of the field of view for understanding at the level required for reading source code. These limitations correspond roughly to the 70 to 80 column range.

2.2   SUMMARY

- Employ a consistent spacing strategy around delimiters.

- Indent and align nested control structures, continuation lines, and embedded units consistently.

- Distinguish between indentation for statement–list structure and for continuation lines.

- Use a series of spaces for indentation, not the tab character.

- Align operators vertically to emphasize local program structure.

- Organize declarations as a table.

- Provide at most one declaration per line.

- Align parameter modes and grouping symbols vertically.

- Use four trailing blanks for mode in and three leading blanks for mode out.

- Use blank lines to group logically related lines of text.

- Mark the top of the body of each program unit and the beginning and end of its frame.

- Mark the top and bottom of a package specification.

- Start each statement on a new line.

- Write no more than one simple statement per line.

- Break compound statements over multiple lines.

- Adhere to a maximum line length limit for source code.

Chapter 3

Readability

This chapter recommends ways of using Ada features in a manner that will enhance the ability to read and understand code. There are many myths about comments and readability. The responsibility for true readability rests more with naming and with code structure than with comments. Having as many comment lines as code lines does not imply readability; it more likely indicates the writer does not understand the code or the problem it is intended to solve.

3.1   SPELLING

Spelling conventions in source code include rules for capitalization, use of underscores, and use of abbreviations. If these conventions are followed consistently, the resulting code will be clearer and more readable.

3.1.1   Use of Underscores

guideline

- Use underscores to separate words in a compound name.

example

```
MILES_PER_HOUR
ENTRY_VALUE
```

rationale

When an identifier consists of more than one word, it is much easier to read if the words are separated by underscores. Indeed, there is precedent in English in which words within a compound word are separated by a hyphen. In addition to promoting readability of the code, if underscores are used in names a code

formatter can transform the code into another format if required.   See also
Guideline 3.1.3.

3.1.2   Numbers ‡

guideline

- Represent numbers in a consistent fashion.

- Represent literals in a radix appropriate to the problem.

- Use underscores to separate digits the same way commas would be used in handwritten text.

- When using scientific notation, make the "e" consistently either upper or lower case.

- In an alternate base, represent the alphabetic characters in either all upper case, or all lower case.

- Use underscores in alternate base numbers in the same way blanks or commas would be used in handwritten text.

example

```
type MAXIMUM_SAMPLES      is range  1          .. 1_000_000;
type LEGAL_HEX_ADDRESS    is range 16#0000#    .. 16#FFFF#;
type LEGAL_OCTAL_ADDRESS is range  8#000_000# .. 8#777_777#;

AVOGADRO_NUMBER : constant := 6.022169E+23;
```

To represent the number 1/3 as a constant,

```
-- use
ONE_THIRD  : constant := 3#0.1#; -- yes, it really works!
-- or
ONE_THIRD  : constant := 1.0/3.0;

-- Avoid this use.
ONE_THIRD  : constant := 0.33333333333333;
```

rationale

Each of these guidelines aids recognition. Consistent use of case aids scanning for numbers. Underscores serve to group portions of numbers into familiar patterns. Consistency with common usage in everyday contexts is a large part of readability.

note

If a rational fraction is represented in a base that is a terminating rather than a repeating decimal representation, then it may contain increased accuracy upon conversion to the machine base.

3.1.3   Capitalization ‡

guideline

- Make reserved words and other elements of the program distinct from each
  other.

example

Reserved words are lower case, identifier names are capitalized:

```
case TIME_OF_DAY is
    when BEFORE_NOON    =>   GET_READY_FOR_LUNCH;
    when HIGH_NOON      =>   EAT_LUNCH;
    when others         =>   GET_TO_WORK;
end case; -- TIME_OF_DAY
```

rationale

Visually distinguishing reserved words allows the reader to focus on program
structure alone if desired and also aids scanning for particular identifiers.

note

Nissen and Wallis ([18] page 2.1) state that "The choice of case is highly
debatable, and that chosen for the Ada LRM is not necessarily the best. The use
of lower case for reserved words is often preferred, so that they do not stand out
too much. However, lower case is generally easier to read than is upper case;
words can be distinguished by their overall shape, and can be found more quickly
when scanning the text."

Ada names are not case sensitive. Therefore the names max_limit, MAX_LIMIT,
and Max_Limit denote the same object or entity. A good code formatter should be
able to automatically convert from one style to another.

Write source code so that it can be reformatted by a code formatter for the
desired style if required. Pick any capitalization style as long as you stick to it and
can convert to the style preferred by management. For ease of entry and editing,
it may be better to use all lower case and have a formatter automatically convert to
the presentation (readable) form for review listings.

3.1.4   Abbreviations

guideline

- Spell out identifiers completely.
- Do not use an abbreviation where a shorter full name is available for a long
  identifier.
- Use a consistent abbreviation strategy.
- Do not use uncommon or ambiguous abbreviations.

- An abbreviation must save many characters over the full word to be justified.
- If a project has accepted abbreviations, maintain a list and use only abbreviations on that list.

example

Use `TIME_OF_RECEIPT` rather than `RECD_TIME` or `R_TIME`

rationale

Abbreviations only serve to aid the developer when entering the code. Many abbreviations are ambiguous or unintelligible unless taken in context. As a simple example, `TEMP` could indicate either temporary or temperature.

note

Moderation is in order. Very long variable names can obscure the structure of the program. This is particularly so in deeply nested (indented) control structures.

For naming conventions that help avoid abbreviations, see Guideline 3.3.1. An abbreviated format for a fully qualified name can be established via the renames clause. This capability is useful when a very long fully qualified name would otherwise occur many times in a localized section of code (see Guideline 5.7.2).

A list of accepted abbreviations for a project provides a standard context for the use of each abbreviation.

3.2   COMMENTARY

Commentary includes all entities within a software component that are in the Ada syntactic form called comments. Commentary can be either beneficial or harmful to software maintainers. We take the position that commentary should be minimized; restricted to comments that emphasize the structure of code and comments that draw attention to deliberate and necessary violations of the guidelines. It is important to note that many of the examples in this book include more commentary than we would generally consider necessary or advisable. It is present either to draw attention to the real issue that is being exemplified, or to compensate for elision or incompleteness in the example program.

Maintenance programmers need to know the causal interaction of non-contiguous pieces of code to get a global, more or less complete sense of the program. They typically garner this kind of information from mental simulation of parts of the code. Commentary should be just sufficient to support this process or render it unnecessary [24].

3.2.1   General Commentary

guideline

- Make comments unnecessary by trying to make the code say everything.

- When in doubt, leave out the comment.

- Do not use commentary to replace or replicate information that should be provided in separate documentation such as design documents.

- Where a comment is required, make it succinct, concise, and grammatically correct.

example

```
   ...
case ...
   ...
   END_OF_FILE_TOKEN =>
      raise UNEXPECTED_END_OF_FILE;
         -- Abandon input scan and code generation.
         -- Skip to error message and listing processing.
```

rationale

The structure and function of well written code should be clear without commentary. Obscure or badly structured code is hard to understand, maintain or reuse irrespective of the amount of commentary; bad code should be improved, not explained. In addition, during maintenance, commentary must be updated along with the code it explains, which is a potential source of inconsistency and error.

The commentary should reveal to a reader only information which is difficult to extract from the program text. Regardless of the particular format or style mandated by a standard or an organization, it will be possible to include too much information in commentary. This is a difficult situation to recognize when you are creating it. Too much information is subject to sudden and frequent change which may go unnoticed by the programmer responsible for the documentation. This is one cause of cascading errors. It also violates the general design principle that information not needed should be hidden.

Information that is extraneous to commentary but necessary for readers or modifiers of the code, (e.g., the calling units for a subprogram) can be generated using tools. As in the case of cross referencing, some information is better generated through tools than programmer generated comments. This applies, for example, to design documentation and revision histories.

The purpose of commentary is to help readers understand the code. Misspelled, ambiguous, misleading, incomplete, scattered, or grammatically incorrect commentary defeats this purpose. Also, a reader will tend to skip over long passages. Review commentary with at least as much care as the code.

3.2.2   File Headers ‡

guideline

- Place in the header of Ada source code only information that will identify important characteristics of the code.

- Include in header comments only what a reader will trust.

- Include copyright notices.

- Include author name(s), dates and place.

- Indicate where to look for implementation and machine dependencies.

example

```
--------------------------------------------------------------------------
-- Author:
-- Date:
-- Department:
-- Phone:
-- Copyright:
-- Dependencies:
--------------------------------------------------------------------------
```

rationale

Readers of source code, particularly maintainers, only trust limited parts of typical header comment blocks. Including other, *de facto* extraneous or superfluous information is a waste of time. Most of the information typically included in header comment blocks is not for readers of the code, but for tools whose purpose is to build design documents after the fact. When present, a copyright notice often subsumes place of origin.

The header information gives readers of the code a history and an introduction to the code if they must maintain it at a later date. The code may be stored in a reusable library. In that case, the revision history, description of the source code, external information (units accessed, etc.) as well as the device input/output, machine and compiler dependencies become very important.

3.2.3   Unit Function Description

guideline

- When describing the functionality of a software component, avoid a restatement of the code itself [26].

- If they are needed at all, the comments in the specification should provide information concerning the interface the unit presents to other parts of the program.

- If they are needed at all, the comments in the body should contain information on how the operations and their formal parameters are used within the unit.

example

```
------------------------------------------------------------------
package HANDLE_ROBOT_DEVICE is

   function DEVICE_NOT_READY return BOOLEAN;
      -- Used to avoid raising the MOVE_WHEN_NOT_READY exception.

   MOVE_WHEN_NOT_READY : exception;
      -- Raised when event sequence is incorrect.

   EXCESS_MOTOR_CURRENT  : exception;
      -- Raised when arm motion too fast.
   LIMIT_SWITCH_CLOSURE  : exception;
      -- Raised when arm position not safe.

   procedure MAKE_READY (...);
   procedure MOVE_ROBOT_DEVICE (...);
   ...
end HANDLE_ROBOT_DEVICE;
------------------------------------------------------------------
```

rationale

If the routine and parameters are named well, there is no need for comments describing their purpose(s). Restating the code is redundant and provides no information that cannot be obtained more reliably by reading the code itself. Further, when the commentary is too similar to the implementation, it can be put out-of-date too easily by minor changes to the code. Often both authors and maintainers overlook these problems.

When a unit does need comments in its specification, these should describe the unit's purpose on its own. Information on its role in the program, such as which other units use it, is superfluous and can become misleading during maintenance.

exceptions

If the code uses a complex algorithm, it could be beneficial to readers to have the algorithm in a pseudo-code version or a reference to a text describing the algorithm included in the comments of the body.

Comments in the specification may be useful in describing the behavior of the subprogram or package to a programmer interested in reusing it, e.g., $O(n \log n)$ time, recursive, may block due to entry calls, accesses global variables. See Guideline 8.2.1.

3.2.4   Marker Comments

guideline

- Make judicious use of marker comments.

- Use pagination markers (Guideline 2.1.7).

- Repeat the unit simple name at the `begin` of a package body, subprogram body, task body, and a block <u>if</u> it is preceded by declarations.

- Mark the end of an if or a case statement and the reserved words `else` and `elsif` with a short form of the conditional expression or other indicator of the purpose accomplished by that point.

example

The `if`, `else`, and `end` `if` of an if statement are usually separated by long sequences of statements, often involving other if statements. Marker comments emphasize the association of the keywords of the same statement over a great visual distance.

```
if B_FOUND then
    -- large statement sequence
else -- B not found
    -- large statement sequence
end if; -- B_FOUND
```

The sequence of statements of a package body is usually very far from the first line of the package. If a package body does have a sequence of statements, it is usually long. The marker comment emphasizes the association of the `begin` with the package.

```
----------------------------------------------------------------------
package body ABSTRACT_STRINGS is
    ... -- many declarations
    ------------------------------------------------------------------
    procedure CATENATE( ... ) is
        ...
    end CATENATE;
    ------------------------------------------------------------------
    ... -- many more subprograms, etc.
    ------------------------------------------------------------------
begin -- ABSTRACT_STRINGS
    ...
end ABSTRACT_STRINGS;
----------------------------------------------------------------------
```

rationale

Marker comments are used to emphasize the structure of code and to make it easier to read. They help the reader in resolving questions about his current position in the code. This is more so for large units than small. A short marker comment will fit on the same line as the reserved word with which it is associated. Thus it will inform without clutter.

Repeating names and noting conditional expressions will clutter the code if overdone. As in the examples, it is visual distance that makes marker comments beneficial.

3.2.5   Highlighting

guideline

- Use commentary to highlight and explain violations of programming guidelines or standards.

- Use commentary to highlight and explain unusual or special code features.

example

Suppose a portion of code uses the assembly language level test and set instruction versus the Ada rendezvous model to perform some sort of synchronization. Make your documentation call attention to the fact. In addition to providing information about the assembly code, give a rationale for not using a higher–level Ada construct. Explain why other methods did not work, e.g. timing requirements were not met.

```
-- Ada does not allow...
-- This block exploits...
```

rationale

Highlighting violations of guidelines or standards, or other unusual or special code features, indicates that they are intentional and intended to achieve some purpose. This assists maintainers by focusing their attention on code sections that are likely to cause problems during maintenance or when porting the program to another implementation.

If you restrict highlighting comments to these situations, the comments you do include will let the reader know you are emphasizing something unusual and that those comments are to be taken seriously.

note

Highlighting or meta comments should be used to document code that is non-portable, implementation-dependent, environment-dependent or tricky in any way. They notify the reader that something unusual was put there for a reason. A beneficial comment would be one explaining a workaround for a compiler bug. If you use a lower level (not "ideal" in the software engineering sense) solution, comment it. Information included in the comments should state why you used that particular construct. Also include documentation of the failed attempts, e.g. using a higher level structure. This type of commentary is useful to maintainers for historical purposes, and helps them avoid "false starts." Show the reader that a significant amount of thought went into the choice of a construct.

3.3   NAMING CONVENTIONS

Choose names which make clear the object's or entity's intended use. Ada allows identifiers to be of any length as long as the identifier fits on a line, with all characters being significant. Identifiers are the names used for variables, constants, program units, and other entities within a program.

3.3.1   Names

guideline

- Choose names that are as nearly self–documenting as possible.

- Choose names that have a unique pronunciation [26].

- Use a short full name instead of an abbreviation (See Guideline 3.1.4).

- Use the context to shorten names.

- Reserve the best name for the variable, and the next best for the type.

- Use names given by the application, but not obscure jargon.

example

TIME_OF_DAY instead of TOD

In a tree-walker, using the name LEFT instead of LEFT_BRANCH is sufficient to convey the full meaning given the context.

rationale

"Self–documenting" names require fewer explanatory comments.   Unique pronunciation for names facilitates human communication and avoids confusion. These attributes can be helpful in comprehending programs. You can further improve comprehension if your variable names are not excessively long ([23] page 7). The context and the application can help greatly. The unit of measure for numeric entities can be a source of names.

note

The acronyms EDT for Eastern Daylight Time, GMT for Greenwich Mean Time, and FFT for Fast Fourier Transform are good names rather than abbreviations. They are commonly accepted and widely used and generally are given by the application. (but see Guideline 8.2.3) Mathematical formulae are often given using single–letter names for variables. Continue this convention for mathematical equations where it would recall the formula e.g.:

A * (X**2) + B * X + C.

3.3.2   Type Identification

guideline

- Choose a name indicative of a category.

- Consider using a plural form as a type name.

- Use specific suffixes.

- If you use suffixes, reserve them only for types.

example

```
_TYPE       -- too generic
_NAME       -- specific for an enumeration
_INFO       -- specific for a record
OPEN_MODE: OPEN_MODES;     -- type name as plural of variable name.
```

rationale

Careful choice of type names clarifies type definitions by conveying meaning about the objects to be declared, and clarifies declarations by indicating the purpose of the declared objects. Using categorical or plural nouns or noun phrases as type names helps to emphasize their generic nature. Suffixes, if used, should be sufficiently specific to convey useful information. Reserving suffixes for type names avoids confusing the reader with object names which are generic in form.

note

Keep in mind the proper level of abstraction so that the information contained in the name will be useful to a reader of an object declaration where only the typemark occurs without the structuring information included in the type definition.   The name should <u>not</u> indicate anything about the structure implementing the type.

Occasionally, it is very difficult to come up with an appropriate categorical name to encompass all the objects of a given type. In such cases, it is better to employ a suffix indicating that a category is intended rather than some word which by itself does not readily suggest a category. If this is the case, use descriptive suffixes such as _CLASS, _KIND, etc. [17] [26]. Be aware that appending the suffix can make declarations awkward and will always make them longer. Mixing uses for suffixes only obscures the intent for the reader.

3.3.3   Object Identification

guideline

- Form object names from words or phrases suggesting objects in natural language.

- Use common nouns for non-boolean objects.

- Use predicate clauses or adjectives for boolean objects.
- If you choose plural forms for type names, use singular forms for objects.

example

Non-boolean objects:
```
    CURRENT_USER       : USER_NAMES;       -- noun
    CLASS_SCHEDULE     : SCHEDULE_TABLES;  -- noun
```

Boolean objects:
```
    USER_IS_AVAILABLE  : BOOLEAN;          -- predicate clause
    LIST_IS_EMPTY      : BOOLEAN;          -- predicate clause
    EMPTY              : BOOLEAN;          -- adjective
    BRIGHT             : BOOLEAN;          -- adjective
```

rationale

By adhering to conventions relating object types and parts of speech, code readability is improved. The use of natural language enables construction of nearly self-documenting code and encourages writing programs which read as much as possible like text.

note

If the program is modeling some action in a domain with previously established naming conventions, use the conventions for the domain since they will be more familiar to readers of the code.

3.3.4   Program Unit Identification

guideline

- Choose names for program units that reflect their level of organization and functionality[17].
- Give procedures and entries identifiers that contain a transitive, imperative verb phrase describing the action.
- Give boolean valued functions predicate-clause names.
- Give non-boolean valued functions noun names.
- Give packages names that imply higher levels of organization than subprograms. Generally, these will be noun phrases that describe the abstraction provided.
- Give tasks names that imply an active entity.
- Name generic subprograms as if they were non-generic subprograms.
- Name generic packages as if they were non-generic packages.
- Make the generic names more general than the instantiated names.

example

1) Sample names for elements that comprise an Ada program.

Sample procedure names:

```
OBTAIN_NEXT_TOKEN    -- obtain is a transitive verb
CREATE_NEW_GROUP     -- create is a transitive verb
```

Sample function names:
    for boolean-valued functions:

```
STACK.IS_EMPTY       -- predicate clause
IS_LAST_ITEM         -- predicate clause
DEVICE_IS_READY      -- predicate clause
```

for non-boolean-valued functions:

```
STACK.TOP            -- common noun with prepositional phrase
                     -- used as adjective
SUCCESSOR            -- common noun
SENSOR.READING       -- common noun participle with adjective
```

Sample package names:

```
TERMINAL_OPERATIONS  -- common noun
TEXT_UTILITIES       -- common noun
```

Sample task names:

```
TERMINAL_RESOURCE_MANAGER -- common noun that shows action
```

2) This example shows code using the parts-of-speech naming conventions. The example takes the guidelines one step further and shows the reader what the program is doing.

```
OBTAIN_NEXT_TOKEN (...);
case CURRENT_TOKEN is
   when IDENTIFIER => PROCESS_IDENTIFIER;
   when NUMERIC    => PROCESS_NUMERIC;
   ...
end case;  -- CURRENT_TOKEN
```

rationale

Use of these naming conventions creates understandable code that reads much like natural language. When verbs are used for actions, such as subprograms, and nouns are used for objects, such as the data that the subprogram manipulates, code is easier to read and understand. This models a medium of communication already familiar to a reader. Where the pieces of a program model a real-life situation, use of these conventions reduces the number of translation steps involved in reading and understanding the program. In a sense, your choice of names reflects the level of abstraction from computer hardware toward application requirements.

note

There are some conflicting conventions in current use for task entries. Some programmers and designers advocate naming task entries with the same conventions used for subprograms to blur the fact that a task is involved. Their reasoning is that if the task is re-implemented as a package, the names need not change. This approach has a similar benefit where a package is re-implemented as a task. Others prefer to make the fact of a task entry as explicit as possible to ensure that the existence of a task with its presumed overhead is recognizable. Program- or project-specific priorities may be useful in choosing between these conventions.

3.3.5   Constants and Named Numbers

guideline

- Use symbolic values wherever possible.
- Use constants and named numbers to identify constant-valued entities.
- Use named numbers in preference to constants when possible.
- Use named numbers to replace numeric literals whose type or context is truly universal.
- Use constants for objects whose values cannot change after elaboration [16] [26].
- Show relationships between symbolic values by defining them with static expressions.
- Use linearly independent sets of literals.
- Use the attributes ´SUCC and ´PRED wherever possible.

example

```
3.141_592_653_589_793                              -- literal
PI : constant FLOAT := 3.141_592_653_589_793; -- constant
PI : constant       := 3.141_592_653_589_793; -- named number
PI / 2                                             -- static expression
PI                                                 -- symbolic value
```

Declaring PI as a named number allows it to be referenced symbolically in the assignment statement below:

```
AREA := PI * RADIUS**2;        -- if radius is known.
-- instead of
AREA := 3.14159 * RADIUS**2;   -- Needs explanatory comment.
```

Also, ASCII.BEL is more expressive than CHARACTER´VAL(8#007#).

Clarity of constant declarations can be improved by using other constants. For example:

```
BYTES_PER_PAGE      : constant := 512;
PAGES_PER_BUFFER    : constant := 10;
BUFFER_SIZE         : constant := PAGES_PER_BUFFER * BYTES_PER_PAGE;

-- is more self-explanatory and safer than

BUFFER_SIZE : constant := 5120;   -- ten pages
```

The following literals should be constants

```
if NEW_CHARACTER = '$' -- magic constant that may change
if CURRENT_COLUMN = 7  -- magic constant that may change
```

rationale

Using identifiers instead of numeric literals or "magic constants" makes the purpose of expressions clear. This lessens the necessity of accompanying expressions with commentary. Constant declarations consisting of expressions of numeric literals are safer since they need not be computed by hand. They are also more enlightening than a single numeric literal since there is more opportunity for embedding explanatory names. Clarity of constant declarations can be improved further by using other related constants in static expressions defining new constants. Static expressions of named numbers are computed with infinite precision at compile time.

A constant has a type; a named number can only be of a universal type: universal integer or universal real. Strong typing is enforced for identifiers but not literals. Named numbers allow compilers to generate more efficient code than for constants and to perform more complete error checking at compile time. If the literal contains a large number of digits (as PI in the example above), the use of an identifier reduces keystroke errors. If keystroke errors occur, they are easier to locate either by inspection or at compile time.

Linear independence of literals means that the few literals that are used do not depend on one another and that any relationship between constant or named values is shown in the static expressions. Linear independence of literal values gives the property that if one literal value changes, all of the named numbers of values dependent on that literal are automatically changed.

The literal 1 often occurs in situations where it could be replaced by the 'SUCC and 'PRED attributes. Where these attributes are used instead of the literal 1, the underlying type can be switched easily during maintenance between numeric and enumeration types. Another benefit of using these attributes is that the operations are more explicit, self-documenting, and instructive than having the maintainer answer such questions as: "If something somewhere else changes, does the 1 change to, say, 5?"

note

> There are some gray areas where the literal is actually more self-documenting than a name. These are application-specific and generally occur with universally familiar, unchangeable values such as the following relationship:

```
FAHRENHEIT := 32.0 + (9.0 / 5.0) * CELSIUS;
```

3.4 USING TYPING

Strong typing promotes reliability in software. The type definition of an object defines all legal values and operations and allows the compiler to check for and identify potential errors during compilation. In addition, the rules of type allow the compiler to generate code to check for violations of type constraints at execution time. Use of these features of Ada compilers facilitates earlier and more complete error detection than the methods available to users of less strongly typed languages.

3.4.1 Declaring Types

guideline

- Limit the range of scalar types as much as possible.
- Seek information about possible values from the application.
- Limit the use of predefined numeric types from package STANDARD.
- Do not overload any of the type names in package STANDARD.
- Use subtype declarations to improve program readability [6].
- Use derived types and subtypes in concert (see Guideline 5.3.1).

example

```
subtype CARD_IMAGE is STRING (1 .. 80);
INPUT_LINE : CARD_IMAGE := (others => ' ');

-- restricted integer type:
type DAY_OF_LEAP_YEAR is range 1 .. 366;
subtype DAY_OF_NON_LEAP_YEAR is DAY_OF_LEAP_YEAR range 1 .. 365;
```

By the following declaration, the programmer means, "I haven't the foggiest idea how many," but the actual range will show up buried in the code or as a system parameter:

```
EMPLOYEE_COUNT : INTEGER;
```

rationale

Eliminating meaningless values from the legal range improves the compiler's ability to detect errors when an object is set to an invalid value. This also improves program readability. In addition, it forces you to think carefully about each use of objects declared to be of the subtype.

Different implementations provide different sets of values for most of the predefined types. A reader cannot determine the intended range from the predefined names. This situation is aggravated when the predefined names are overloaded.

The names of an object and its subtype can make clear their intended use and document low-level design decisions. The example above documents a design decision to restrict the software to devices whose physical parameters are derived from the characteristics of Hollerith cards. This information is easy to find for any later changes, enhancing program maintainability.

Declaration of a subtype without a constraint is the method for renaming a type ([28] §8.5).

Types can have highly constrained sets of values without eliminating useful values. Usage as described in Guideline 5.3.1 eliminates many flag variables and type conversions within executable statements. This renders the program more readable while allowing the compiler to enforce strong typing constraints.

note

Subtype declarations do not define new types, only constraints for existing types.

Recognize that any deviation from this guideline will detract from advantages to be had from the strong typing facilities of the Ada language.

3.4.2   Enumeration Types

guideline

- Use enumeration types instead of numeric encodings.
- Use representation clauses to match requirements of external devices.

example

```
-- Use
type COLORS is (
    BLUE,       RED,
    GREEN,      YELLOW
    );

-- rather than

BLUE : constant := 1;
RED  : constant := 2;
   ...
```

rationale

Enumerations are more robust than encodings; they leave less potential for errors resulting from incorrect interpretation, and from additions to and deletions from the set of values during maintenance. Encodings are holdovers from languages that have no user−defined types.

In addition, Ada provides a number of attributes ('POS, 'VAL, 'SUCC, 'PRED, 'IMAGE, and 'VALUE) for enumeration types which, when used, are more reliable than user−written operations on encodings.

An encoding might at first seem appropriate to be certain that specific values match requirements for signals on control lines or expected inputs from sensors. These situations instead call for a representation clause on the enumeration type (examples can be found in §13.3 of the Ada LRM [28]). The representation clause documents the "encoding" and, if the program is properly structured to isolate and encapsulate hardware dependencies (see Guideline 7.1.6) will end up in its proper place. That proper place is an interface package where the "encoding" values can be found and replaced easily should the requirements change.

3.4.3 Overloaded Enumeration Literals

guideline

- Do not overload enumeration literals.

- If you must overload them, qualify all references.

example

```
type TRAFFIC_SIGNAL is (
    RED,        AMBER,
    GREEN
    );

type COLOR_SPECTRUM is (
    RED,        ORANGE,
    YELLOW,     GREEN,
    BLUE,       INDIGO,
    VIOLET
    );

CURRENT_SIGNAL_COLOR : TRAFFIC_SIGNAL;
CURRENT_LIGHT_COLOR  : COLOR_SPECTRUM;
...

-- qualify references to the overloaded literals as follows:
VALUE := TRAFFIC_SIGNAL'(RED)
VALUE := COLOR_SPECTRUM'(RED)
...
```

rationale

In most cases, your compiler will be able to resolve the overloading correctly. This will not be so easy for you or for readers of the code. Specific compilers may not be able to resolve some cases. Such ambiguity can lead to incorrect assumptions which can lead to incorrect actions on your part as author of a program under construction or on the part of maintainers modifying the program. Wherever it is not immediately obvious to which type a literal belongs, you can be making a mistake. If the same literal never appears in more than one enumeration, these problems cannot occur.

exception

If you cannot avoid overloading enumeration types, make sure that all references to the overloaded literals are fully qualified, as illustrated above.

3.5   SUMMARY

spelling

- Use underscores to separate words in a compound name.

- Represent numbers in a consistent fashion.

- Represent literals in a radix appropriate to the problem.

- Use underscores to separate digits the same way commas would be used in handwritten text.

- When using scientific notation, make the "e" consistently either upper or lower case.

- In an alternate base, represent the alphabetic characters in either all upper case, or all lower case.

- Use underscores in alternate base numbers in the same way blanks or commas would be used in handwritten text.

- Make reserved words and other elements of the program distinct from each other.

- Spell out identifiers completely.

- Do not use an abbreviation where a shorter full name is available for a long identifier.

- Use a consistent abbreviation strategy.

- Do not use uncommon or ambiguous abbreviations.

- An abbreviation must save many characters over the full word to be justified.

- If a project has accepted abbreviations, maintain a list and use only abbreviations on that list.

commentary

- Make comments unnecessary by trying to make the code say everything.

- When in doubt, leave out the comment.

- Do not use commentary to replace or replicate information that should be provided in separate documentation such as design documents.

- Where a comment is required, make it succinct, concise, and grammatically correct.

- Place in the header of Ada source code only information that will identify important characteristics of the code.

- Include in header comments only what a reader will trust.

- Include copyright notices.

- Include author name(s), dates and place.

- Indicate where to look for implementation and machine dependencies.

- When describing the functionality of a software component, avoid a restatement of the code itself.

- If they are needed at all, the comments in the specification should provide information concerning the interface the unit presents to other parts of the program.

- If they are needed at all, the comments in the body should contain information on how the operations and their formal parameters are used within the unit.

- Make judicious use of marker comments.

- Use pagination markers.

- Repeat the unit simple name at the `begin` of a package body, subprogram body, task body, and a block <u>if</u> it is preceded by declarations.

- Mark the end of an if or a case statement and the reserved words `else` and `elsif` with a short form of the conditional expression or other indicator of the purpose accomplished by that point.

- Use commentary to highlight and explain violations of programming guidelines or standards.

- Use commentary to highlight and explain unusual or special code features.

naming conventions

- Choose names that are as nearly self-documenting as possible.

- Choose names that have a unique pronunciation.

- Use a short full name instead of an abbreviation.

- Use the context to shorten names.

- Reserve the best name for the variable, and the next best for the type.

- Use names given by the application, but not obscure jargon.

- Choose a name indicative of a category.

- Consider using a plural form as a type name.

- Use specific suffixes.

- If you use suffixes, reserve them only for types.

- Form object names from words or phrases suggesting objects in natural language.

- Use common nouns for non-boolean objects.

- Use predicate clauses or adjectives for boolean objects.

- If you choose plural forms for type names, use singular forms for objects.

- Choose names for program units that reflect their level of organization and functionality.

- Give procedures and entries identifiers that contain a transitive, imperative verb phrase describing the action.

- Give boolean valued functions predicate–clause names.

- Give non–boolean valued functions noun names.

- Give packages names that imply higher levels of organization than subprograms. Generally, these will be noun phrases that describe the abstraction provided.

- Give tasks names that imply an active entity.

- Name generic subprograms as if they were non–generic subprograms.

- Name generic packages as if they were non–generic packages.

- Make the generic names more general than the instantiated names.

- Use symbolic values wherever possible.

- Use constants and named numbers to identify constant-valued entities.

- Use named numbers in preference to constants when possible.

- Use named numbers to replace numeric literals whose type or context is truly universal.

- Use constants for objects whose values cannot change after elaboration.

- Show relationships between symbolic values by defining them with static expressions.

- Use linearly independent sets of literals.

- Use the attributes ´SUCC and ´PRED wherever possible.

using typing

- Limit the range of scalar types as much as possible.

- Seek information about possible values from the application.

- Limit the use of predefined numeric types from package STANDARD.

- Do not overload any of the type names in package STANDARD.

- Use subtype declarations to improve program readability.

- Use derived types and subtypes in concert.

- Use enumeration types instead of numeric encodings.

- Use representation clauses to match requirements of external devices.

- Do not overload enumeration literals.

- If you must overload them, qualify all references.

Chapter 4

Program Structure

Proper structure improves program clarity. This is akin to readability on lower levels and facilitates the use of the readability guidelines (Chapter 3). The various program structuring facilities provided by Ada were designed to enhance overall clarity of design. These guidelines show how to use these facilities for their intended purposes.

Abstraction and encapsulation are supported by the package concept. Related subprograms can be grouped together and seen by a higher level as a single entity. Information hiding is enforced via strong typing and by the separation of package and subprogram specifications from their respective bodies. Additional language elements that form the unique combination of features within Ada include exception handling and tasking.

4.1 HIGH–LEVEL STRUCTURE

Program structure can have a significant effect on maintainability. Well–structured programs are easily understood, enhanced, and maintained. Poorly structured programs are frequently restructured during maintenance just to make the maintenance job easier. Many of the guidelines listed below are often given as general program design guidelines.

4.1.1   Separate Compilation Capabilities

guideline

- Place a package specification and its body in different files.

- Put as much as is practicable of the subunit structure within the same file as the parent's body.

- Consider placing large subunits or task bodies in separate files.

- Consider providing a specification in a separate file for subprogram library units.

- Use a consistent file naming convention.

example

The file names below illustrate one possible file organization and associated consistent naming convention. The library unit name is used for the body. A trailing underscore indicates the specification, and any files containing subunits use names constructed by separating the body name from the subunit name with two underscores.

```
TEXT_IO_.ADA                      -- the specification
TEXT_IO.ADA                       -- the body
TEXT_IO__INTEGER_IO.ADA           -- a subunit
TEXT_IO__FIXED_IO.ADA             -- a subunit
TEXT_IO__FLOAT_IO.ADA             -- a subunit
TEXT_IO__ENUMERATION_IO.ADA       -- a subunit
```

rationale

Separate compilation capabilities reduce complexity for the human reader, but they can be abused. Physical separation of specification and body enhances the sense of their logical separation. Separation can also help prevent internal objects from making their way into the specification by accident. Using separate files for specification and body provides for different bodies with differing size vs. speed tradeoffs or for different bodies specific to different machines.

Separating subunits out from a body is similarly desirable. This can be done within the same file. Using multiple files for all subunits is excessive. Maintainers and others who read code can focus more easily on smaller pieces, yet they are also better able to grasp a package as a whole if it is entirely located together.

In large programs, using the same file for all parts of a body can waste development time since a change in a single subunit then requires recompilation of the parent and all its children. This calls for tradeoffs in following this guideline.

Large subunits should generally be in separate files. The physical separation then emphasizes the conceptual complexity and importance of the subunit relative to its parent. Task bodies are also candidates for separate files, given the conceptual model of a separate program with its own virtual processor (see Guideline 6.1.1).

During development, some subunits may be transiently in a less complete state than other subunits or their parent. In such cases it is often convenient to start with them in different files, irrespective of size, deferring the decision as to their eventual location. If they are still small when complete, they can be put back into the same file as the parent, but remain subunits. If they are large, they can be left in separate files. The overall objective should be to achieve an appropriate balance of the opposing goals of minimizing the number of files and improving clarity by physical separation.

Providing an (optional) subprogram specification for a subprogram library unit allows the body to be recompiled without invalidating its callers.

Where there are many files associated with a program unit, a consistent file naming convention can reduce apparent file system clutter. Still, this cannot help with a superfluity of files. Library units so large that no satisfactory balance between the number of files and their size is achievable may reflect poor design.

4.1.2   Subprograms

guideline

- Use subprograms to enhance abstraction.
- Use the pragma INLINE where call overhead is of paramount concern.
- Restrict each subprogram to the performance of a single action [17].

example

Your program is required to output text to many types of devices. Since the devices would accept a variety of character sets, the proper way to do this is to write a subprogram to convert to the required character set within the subprogram that writes out the data. This way, the output subprogram has one purpose and the conversions are done elsewhere.

```
--------------------------------------------------------------------------
procedure OUTPUT_TO_DEVICE (OUTPUT_DATA : in    TEXT_DATA;
                            DEVICE      : in    DEVICE_TYPE;
                            STATUS      :   out ERROR_CODES) is
   -- local declarations
begin -- OUTPUT_TO_DEVICE
   ...
   case DEVICE.CHARACTER_SET is
      when LIMITED_ASCII  =>
         CONVERT_TO_UPPER_CASE (ORIGINAL_DATA   => OUTPUT_DATA,
                                UPPER_CASE_DATA => UPPER_OUTPUT_DATA);

      when EXTENDED_ASCII =>
         ...
      when EBCDIC         =>
         ...
   end case; -- DEVICE_TYPE.CHARACTER_SET
   ...
end OUTPUT_TO_DEVICE;
--------------------------------------------------------------------------
```

rationale

Subprograms are an extremely effective and well–understood abstraction technique. Subprograms increase program readability by hiding the details of a particular activity. It is not necessary that a subprogram be called more than once to justify its existence.

The case statement in the example is more readable and understandable with the bodies of the conversion routines elsewhere, and the judicious choice of subprogram names has enhanced the understanding of the purpose of the case statement (see Guideline 3.3.4).

note

In special cases there can be a combination of factors that render a subprogram solution inefficient (e.g., stringent timing constraints and a small subprogram such that the calling overhead takes more time than execution of the subprogram itself). When this happens, maintain the scope, visibility, and information hiding that a subprogram provides by using the pragma INLINE.

4.1.3   Functions

guideline

- When writing a function, make sure it has no side effects.
- If a subprogram involves a conceptually large computation, make it a procedure.

rationale

A side effect is a change to any variable that is not local to the subprogram. This includes changes to variables by other subprograms and entries during calls from the function if the changes will persist after the function returns. Although the Ada language permits functions to have side effects, they can sometimes lead to problems with incorrect order dependencies. Discourage using side effects anywhere.

Although functions can be called from within expressions allowing freedom of expression and supporting readable code, using a procedure rather than a function can call attention to the use of a large computation located elsewhere. This enhances readability since the call is not buried within an expression.

exceptions

There are a very few cases in which functions having side effects is accepted practice. One such case is a random number generator. Others, such as recording performance analysis data or information for recovery, have little to do with the application.

4.1.4   Packages

guideline

- Use packages for information hiding and abstract data types.

- Use packages to model abstract entities appropriate to the problem domain.

- Use packages to group together related type and object declarations (e.g., common declarations for two or more library units).

- Use packages to group together related program units for configuration control or visibility reasons [17].

- Use packages to group together related declarations and components for later reuse.

- Encapsulate machine dependencies in packages. Place a software interface to a particular device in a package to facilitate a change to a different device.

- Place low-level implementation decisions or interfaces in subprograms within packages. The pragma INLINE can be used to remove subprogram calling overhead.

- Use packages and subprograms to encapsulate and hide program details that may change [18].

example

A package called BACKING_STORAGE_INTERFACE could contain type and subprogram declarations to support a generalized view of an external memory system (such as a disk or a drum). Its internals may, in turn, be dependent on other more hardware- or operating-system-specific packages.

rationale

Packages are the principal structuring facility in Ada. They are intended to be used as direct support for abstraction, information hiding, and modularization. For example, they are useful for encapsulating machine dependencies as an aid to portability. A single specification can have multiple bodies isolating implementation-specific information so other parts of the code need not change.

Encapsulating areas of potential change helps to minimize the effort required to implement that change by preventing unnecessary dependencies among unrelated parts of the system.

4.1.5   Functional Cohesion

guideline

- Make each package serve a single purpose.
- Use packages to group <u>functionally</u> related data, types, and subprograms.
- Avoid collections of unrelated objects and subprograms [17][18].

example

The following package is obviously a "catch all" for a particular project and is likely to be a jumbled mess. It probably has this form to permit project members to incorporate a single with clause into their software.

```
package PROJECT_DEFINITIONS is
```

The following package contains all the types and constants needed by some specific display associated with some specific device. This is a good example of collecting related information.

```
package DISPLAY_FORMAT_DEFINITIONS is
```

Packages can, and should, be used to collect types, data, and subprograms. The following package provides all the functionality needed to deal with a special purpose device.

```
package CARTRIDGE_TAPE_HANDLER is
```

rationale

See also Guideline 5.4.1 on Heterogeneous Data.

The degree to which the entities in a package are related has a direct impact on the ease of understanding packages and programs made up of packages. There are different criteria for grouping, and some criteria are less effective than others. Grouping the class of data or activity (e.g., initialization modules), and grouping data or activities based on their temporal proximity, are less effective than grouping based on function or need to communicate through data. ([7] paraphrased).

note

Traditional subroutine libraries often group functionally unrelated subroutines. Even such libraries should be broken into a collection of packages each containing a logically cohesive set of subprograms.

4.1.6 Data Coupling

guideline

- Do not share data between packages.

example

This is part of a compiler. Both the package handling error messages and the package containing the code generator need to know the current line number. Rather than storing this in a shared variable of type NATURAL, the information is stored in a package that hides the details of how such information is represented, and makes it available with access functions.

```
-----------------------------------------------------------------------
package COMPILATION_STATUS is
    function SOURCE_LINE_NUMBER return LINE_RANGE;
end COMPILATION_STATUS;
-----------------------------------------------------------------------
with COMPILATION_STATUS;
package ERROR_MESSAGE_PROCESSING is
    -- Handle compile-time diagnostic.
end ERROR_MESSAGE_PROCESSING;
-----------------------------------------------------------------------
with COMPILATION_STATUS;
package CODE_GENERATION is
    -- Operations for code generation.
end CODE_GENERATION;
-----------------------------------------------------------------------
```

rationale

Strongly coupled program units can be difficult to debug and very difficult to maintain. If relationships exist that are either not intentional or not documented properly, the maintainability of the code suffers.

4.1.7 Tasks

guideline

- Use tasks to model abstract, asynchronous entities within the problem domain.

- Use tasks to control or synchronize access to tasks or other asynchronous entities (e.g., asynchronous I/O, peripheral devices, interrupts).

- Use tasks to define concurrent algorithms for multiprocessor architectures.

- Use tasks to perform cyclic or prioritized activities [17].

rationale

The rationale for this guideline is given under Guideline 6.1.1. Chapter 6 deals with tasking in more detail.

4.2   VISIBILITY

Ada's ability to enforce information hiding and separation of concerns through its visibility controlling features is one of the most important advantages of the language, particularly when "programming–in–the–large" where a team of programmers are producing a large system. Subverting these features, for example by excessive reliance on the use clause, is wasteful and dangerous. See also Section 5.7.

4.2.1   Minimization of Interfaces

guideline

- Put only what is needed for the use of a package into its specification.

- Minimize the declaration of objects in package specifications [18].

- Do not include extra operations simply because they are easy to build.

- Minimize the context (with) clauses in a package specification.

- Minimize the number of parameters to subprograms.

- Do not manipulate global data within a subprogram or package merely to limit the number of parameters.

- Avoid unnecessary visibility; hide the implementation details of a program unit from its users.

example

```
--------------------------------------------------------------------
package TELEPHONE_BOOK is

   type NAME_DATA is private;
   -- Operators for the NAME_DATA type follow.  This type is made available
   --  because it is used in other contexts. Note that it is a private type
   -- to limit operations on such objects.
   procedure SET_NAME(...);

   -- Operators for the telephone database itself.  Details of the record
   -- format are totally hidden because the type is defined in the
   -- package body.  This record type is not needed elsewhere.
   procedure INSERT_ENTRY;
   procedure DELETE_ENTRY;
   --------------------------------------------------------------------
private
   type NAME_DATA is record
                      -- field information;
                   end record;
end TELEPHONE_BOOK;
--------------------------------------------------------------------
package body TELEPHONE_BOOK is

   ENTRY_DATA : -- full details of phone record;
   ...
   --------------------------------------------------------------------
   procedure INSERT_ENTRY is
   begin
      ...
   end INSERT_ENTRY;
   --------------------------------------------------------------------
   procedure DELETE_ENTRY is
   begin
      ...
   end DELETE_ENTRY;
   --------------------------------------------------------------------
end TELEPHONE_BOOK;
--------------------------------------------------------------------
```

rationale

Extra information in a package specification wastes maintenance effort. If too much information is given, a user of the package can easily "break" it by changing some of the data so that the group of values is inconsistent. A maintainer must find every use of any part of this package to be sure that it is not being abused.

The fewer the extraneous details, the more understandable the program, package, or subprogram. It is important to maintainers to know exactly what a package interface is so that they can understand the effects of changes. Interfaces to a subprogram extend beyond the parameters; any modification of global data from within a package or subprogram is an undocumented interface to the "outside" as well.

Pushing as many as possible of the context dependencies into the body makes the reader's job easier, localizes the recompilation required when library units change, and helps prevent a ripple effect during modifications. See also Guideline 4.2.3.

Subprograms with large numbers of parameters often indicate poor design decisions (e.g., that the functional boundaries of the subprogram are inappropriate, or that parameters are structured poorly).

Objects visible within package specifications can be modified by any unit that has visibility to them. The object cannot be protected or represented abstractly by its enclosing package. Objects which must persist should be declared in package bodies. Objects whose value depends on program units external to their enclosing package are probably either in the wrong package or are better accessed by a subprogram specified in the package specification.

note

The guideline does not say "eliminate the declaration of objects ..." Some package specifications will be composed entirely of object (and constant) declarations. The goals are to keep as much as possible hidden within the package body or the private part of the package specification and to export only what is necessary for another unit to use the package properly. Visibility of objects such as DEFAULT_WIDTH in package TEXT_IO.INTEGER_IO is useful.

The specifications of some packages, such as in subroutine libraries, cannot be significantly reduced in size. A heuristic is to break these up into smaller packages, grouping according to category, e.g., Trigonometric functions.

4.2.2 Nested Packages

guideline

- Avoid nesting package specifications within package specifications.

- Nest package specifications only for grouping operations, hiding common implementation details, or presenting different views of the same abstraction.

example

The Ada LRM [28] gives an example of desirable package specification nesting. The specifications of generic packages INTEGER_IO, FLOAT_IO, FIXED_IO, and ENUMERATION_IO are nested within the specification of package TEXT_IO. Each of them is a generic, grouping closely related operations and needing to use hidden details of the implementation of TEXT_IO.

rationale

Packages can be nested to reflect levels of abstraction. "When a package provides a good abstraction, it hides the details of its implementation." ([17] page 7–3). When you embed one package specification inside another, it is likely that you are exposing too much information or that the enclosing package is not a good abstraction. Generally, subpackages should be hidden in package bodies rather than exposed in the specifications.

There are valid program structures requiring nesting of package specifications. These are relatively rare.

Where a set of facilities is used by more than one package, but must itself be guaranteed invisible elsewhere, the set of facilities and its users have to be encapsulated in an outer, containing package. In this case, the specifications of the using packages must be nested in the specification of the containing package to make them externally visible (This was the case with TEXT_IO). If the set of facilities supports the implementation of closely related packages, the grouping then also emphasizes the closeness of the original packages' relationship.

note

The nesting of specifications, as in TEXT_IO, provides the needed access and restrictions. Other organizations, such as exporting the common set of facilities from a separate package to be used as context ("with'ed") by the original packages (e.g., FLOAT_IO), are unenforceable.

An abstraction occasionally needs to present different views to different classes of users. Building one view upon another as an additional abstraction does not always suffice, because the functionality of the operations presented by the views may be only partially disjoint. Nesting specifications groups the facilities of the various views, yet associates them with the abstraction they present. Abusive mixing of the views by another unit would be easy to detect due to the multiple use clauses or an incongruous mix of qualified names.

This book cannot provide a complete treatise on program design. The first bullet of this guideline addresses the majority of situations.

4.2.3 Restricting Visibility

guideline

- Restrict the visibility of program units as much as possible [18].
- Minimize the scope within which with clauses apply.
- Compile in the context of (with) only those units directly needed.

example

This program is a compiler. Access to the printing facilities of TEXT_IO is restricted to the software involved in producing the source code listing.

```
--------------------------------------------------------------------
procedure COMPILER is
    --------------------------------------------------------------
    package LISTING_FACILITIES is

        procedure NEW_PAGE_OF_LISTING;
        procedure NEW_LINE_OF_PRINT;
        -- etc.

    end LISTING_FACILITIES;
    --------------------------------------------------------------
    package body LISTING_FACILITIES  is separate;
    --------------------------------------------------------------
begin -- COMPILER
    . . .
end COMPILER;
--------------------------------------------------------------------
with TEXT_IO;
    separate (COMPILER)
package body LISTING_FACILITIES is
    --------------------------------------------------------------
    procedure NEW_PAGE_OF_LISTING is
    begin

        . . .
    end NEW_PAGE_OF_LISTING;
    --------------------------------------------------------------
    procedure NEW_LINE_OF_PRINT is
    begin

        . . .
    end NEW_LINE_OF_PRINT;
    --------------------------------------------------------------
    -- etc

end LISTING_FACILITIES;
--------------------------------------------------------------------
```

rationale

Restricting visibility to a library unit tells maintainers that they need only beware of its use in a localized section. This clarifies exactly what is required for visibility. Code structured in this way is also easier to upgrade.

note

One way to minimize the coverage of a with clause is to use it only with subunits that really need it. When the need for visibility to a library unit is restricted to a subprogram or two, consider making them subunits.

4.2.4　Hiding Tasks

guideline

- Do not include task specifications in package specifications.

- Hide (mask) the fact of a tasking implementation by exporting subprograms that call entries [17] [18].

example

```
---------------------------------------------------------------------
package DISK_HEAD_SCHEDULER is
   type TRACK_NUMBER is ...
   type WORDS is ...
   ------------------------------------------------------------------
   procedure TRANSMIT(TRACK : TRACK_NUMBER;
                      DATA  : WORDS);
   ------------------------------------------------------------------
   ...
end DISK_HEAD_SCHEDULER;
---------------------------------------------------------------------
package body DISK_HEAD_SCHEDULER is
   ...
   ------------------------------------------------------------------
   task CONTROL is
      entry SIGN_IN(TRACK : TRACK_NUMBER);
      ...
   end CONTROL;
   ------------------------------------------------------------------
   task TRACK_MANAGER is
      entry TRANSFER(TRACK_NUMBER)(DATA : WORDS);
   end TRACK_MANAGER;
   ------------------------------------------------------------------
   ...
   ------------------------------------------------------------------
   procedure TRANSMIT(TRACK : TRACK_NUMBER;
                      DATA  : WORDS) is
   begin
      CONTROL.SIGN_IN(TRACK);
      TRACK_MANAGER.TRANSFER(TRACK)(DATA);
   end TRANSMIT;
   ------------------------------------------------------------------
   ...
end DISK_HEAD_SCHEDULER;
---------------------------------------------------------------------
```

rationale

A change to or from a tasking implementation, or a reorganization of services among tasks need not concern users of the package. This guideline supports information hiding and strengthens the abstraction of the enclosing package. Where performance is an issue, the pragma INLINE can be used with the interface subprograms, or the entries can be renamed as subprograms if there are no ordering rules to enforce (see below).

Leaving a task specification in a package body and exporting, via subprograms, only those entries required reduces the amount of extraneous information in the package specification. It allows your subprograms to enforce any order of entry calls necessary to the proper operation of the tasks. This also allows you to impose, on those subprograms, defensive task communication practices (See Guideline 6.2.1) and proper use of conditional and timed entry calls.

Hiding tasks and exporting subprograms calling their entries allows the concealment of entries that should not be made public (e.g., initialization, completion, signals), or the grouping of sets of entries for export to different classes of users (e.g., producers versus consumers). See also Guideline 4.2.2.

note

This guideline provides for hiding the fact of a tasking implementation of a package, grouping some entries and hiding others, package–implementor enforcement of call orders, package–implementor imposition of defensive task communication practices, and package–implementor imposition of proper use of timed and conditional entry calls. With these tools at hand, it is the package implementor's responsibility to ensure that users of the package will not have to concern themselves with behaviors such as deadlock, starvation, and race conditions with respect to the package. If the package user must still know about the tasking implementation to reason about global tasking behavior, comments may be placed in the package specification stating that there is a tasking implementation, describing when a call may block, etc.

This guideline refers only to export of tasks from packages. Do not interpret this guideline as proscribing tasks within subprograms, within other tasks, or wholly contained within package bodies.

4.3   EXCEPTIONS

This section addresses the issue of exceptions in the context of program structures. More material on the use of exceptions is to be found in Section 5.8.

4.3.1   Exported Exceptions

guideline

- Use an exception to indicate an explicit misuse.
- Do not borrow an exception name from another context.

example

```
------------------------------------------------------------------------
package STACK is

    function STACK_EMPTY return BOOLEAN;
        -- Used to avoid raising the NO_DATA_ON_STACK exception.

    NO_DATA_ON_STACK : exception;
        -- Raised when POP used on empty stack. This exception should only be
        -- raised from within this package. The name is exported to allow
        -- handlers to be written by users of this package.

    procedure POP (...);
    procedure PUSH (...);

end STACK;
------------------------------------------------------------------------
```

rationale

There are two reasons a package may export exceptions. The first reason is to make visible to a user a specific indicator of how its facilities have been misused. The exception is to be raised only within the body of the declaring package and to be handled by units that make use of that package. The second reason is to make available to users of proffered types and objects an associated vocabulary for communicating about anomalous situations concerning those types and objects. If the latter form is used, the package might not be providing the best abstraction. Be careful in distinguishing between the two. A rule of thumb is to look at the context of the package specification. A package providing operations is more likely to export an exception for the first reason than for the second. In the first case, be prepared to handle the exception rather than raise it. If the name is not declared in the package's visible part, the exception can only be handled as others if propagated outside.

4.3.2 Abstractions and Exceptions

guideline

- Provide a way to avoid raising an exception.

- Provide a different exception name for each way a package's abstraction can be misused. Raise only that exception for that misuse. Do not raise that exception elsewhere.

- If use of a subprogram can raise an exception, export the name of that exception, i.e., make it visible to any caller.

- Export exceptions at the right level of abstraction. Use them to enhance abstraction.

- Never let an exception escape the boundaries of its abstraction.

- Exceptions are side effects of Ada units and should be documented as such.

example

```
------------------------------------------------------------------
package HANDLE_ROBOT_DEVICE is

    function DEVICE_NOT_READY return boolean;
        -- Used to avoid raising the MOVE_WHEN_NOT_READY exception.

    -- The following exception raised when abstraction misused.
    MOVE_WHEN_NOT_READY : exception;
        -- Raised when event sequence is incorrect.

    -- The following exceptions are part of the abstraction.
    EXCESS_MOTOR_CURRENT  : exception;
        -- Raised when arm motion too fast.
    LIMIT_SWITCH_CLOSURE  : exception;
        -- Raised when arm position not safe.

    procedure MAKE_READY (...);
    procedure MOVE_ROBOT_DEVICE (...);
    --
        -- Other necessary facilities.

end HANDLE_ROBOT_DEVICE;
------------------------------------------------------------------
```

rationale

If there are any kind of boundary conditions for an abstract data type, a user may brush up against them from time to time. Exceptions should be reserved for disastrous occurrences, not as a way of informing the user of the abstraction that a boundary condition has been reached. Providing an interrogative operation, such as the END_OF_FILE function in package TEXT_IO, allows the user to ask whether proceeding will overstep the boundary conditions and raise an exception.

Using specific exception names for the various potential misuses of the abstraction enables the user of the abstraction to determine what was done wrong and to effect appropriate recovery.

Once an exception is propagated outside the scope of the declaration of its name, only a handler for others can catch it. As discussed under Guideline 5.8.3, a handler for others cannot be written to deal with the specific error effectively.

A reader and user of an abstraction needs help establishing conceptual associations between a given operation and the possible exception(s) resulting from its use. Naming the exceptions exported by the abstraction so that they seem naturally associated with the facilities the abstraction provides enhances the abstraction. If an exception is exported that does not have such an association, it probably should have been handled or converted within the implementation of the abstraction rather than being exported.

If you are writing an abstraction, remember that your user will not know about the units you are using in your implementation. That is an effect of information hiding. If any exception is raised within your abstraction, you must catch and handle it. Your user will not be able to provide a reasonable handler if the original exception is allowed to propagate out. You can still convert the exception (see Guideline 5.8.2) into a form intelligible to your user if your abstraction cannot effect recovery on its own.

It is often difficult for a reader to discern which exceptions can be raised as a result of using a program unit. The situation is analogous to side–effects (changes in variables that are not passed as explicit parameters). In this case, the change is to the program counter or execution path of the caller. Exceptions, like side–effects, are difficult to track down in source text and are very undesirable as surprises at execution time. So, be sure to document any exceptions that are not handled by a unit you write.

4.4   SUMMARY

high–level structure

- Place a package specification and its body in different files.
- Put as much as is practicable of the subunit structure within the same file as the parent's body.
- Consider placing large subunits or task bodies in separate files.
- Consider providing a specification in a separate file for subprogram library units.
- Use a consistent file naming convention.
- Use subprograms to enhance abstraction.
- Use the pragma INLINE where call overhead is of paramount concern.
- Restrict each subprogram to the performance of a single action.
- When writing a function, make sure it has no side effects.
- If a subprogram involves a conceptually large computation, make it a procedure.
- Use packages for information hiding and abstract data types.
- Use packages to model abstract entities appropriate to the problem domain.
- Use packages to group together related type and object declarations (e.g., common declarations for two or more library units).

- Use packages to group together related program units for configuration control or visibility reasons.

- Use packages to group together related declarations and components for later reuse.

- Encapsulate machine dependencies in packages. Place a software interface to a particular device in a package to facilitate a change to a different device.

- Place low–level implementation decisions or interfaces in subprograms within packages. The pragma INLINE can be used to remove subprogram calling overhead.

- Use packages and subprograms to encapsulate and hide program details that may change.

- Make each package serve a single purpose.

- Use packages to group functionally related data, types, and subprograms.

- Avoid collections of unrelated objects and subprograms.

- Do not share data between packages.

- Use tasks to model abstract, asynchronous entities within the problem domain.

- Use tasks to control or synchronize access to tasks or other asynchronous entities (e.g., asynchronous I/O, peripheral devices, interrupts).

- Use tasks to define concurrent algorithms for multiprocessor architectures.

- Use tasks to perform cyclic or prioritized activities.

visibility

- Put only what is needed for the use of a package into its specification.

- Minimize the declaration of objects in package specifications.

- Do not include extra operations simply because they are easy to build.

- Minimize the context (with) clauses in a package specification.

- Minimize the number of parameters to subprograms.

- Do not manipulate global data within a subprogram or package merely to limit the number of parameters.

- Avoid unnecessary visibility; hide the implementation details of a program unit from its users.

- Avoid nesting package specifications within package specifications.

- Nest package specifications only for grouping operations, hiding common implementation details, or presenting different views of the same abstraction.

- Restrict the visibility of program units as much as possible.

- Minimize the scope within which with clauses apply.
- Compile in the context of (with) only those units directly needed.
- Do not include task specifications in package specifications.
- Hide (mask) the fact of a tasking implementation by exporting subprograms that call entries.

exceptions

- Use an exception to indicate an explicit misuse.
- Do not borrow an exception name from another context.
- Provide a way to avoid raising an exception.
- Provide a different exception name for each way a package's abstraction can be misused. Raise only that exception for that misuse. Do not raise that exception elsewhere.
- If use of a subprogram can raise an exception, export the name of that exception, i.e., make it visible to any caller.
- Export exceptions at the right level of abstraction. Use them to enhance abstraction.
- Never let an exception escape the boundaries of its abstraction.
- Exceptions are side effects of Ada units and should be documented as such.

Chapter 5

Programming Practices

Software is always subject to change. The need for this change, euphemistically known as "maintenance" arises from a variety of sources. Errors need to be corrected as they are discovered. System functionality may need to be enhanced in planned or unplanned ways. And, inevitably, the requirements change over the lifetime of the system, forcing continual system evolution. Often, these modifications are conducted long after the software was originally written, usually by someone other then the original author.

Easy and successful modification requires that the software be readable, understandable, and structured according to accepted practice. If a software component cannot be understood easily by a programmer who is familiar with its intended function, that software component is not maintainable. Techniques that make code readable and comprehensible enhance its maintainability. So far, we have visited such techniques as consistent use of naming conventions, clear and well-organized commentary, and proper modularization. We now present consistent and logical use of language features.

Reliability is a measure of a program's correctness. While style guidelines cannot enforce the use of correct algorithms, they can suggest the use of techniques and language features known to reduce the number or likelihood of failures. Such techniques include program construction methods that reduce the likelihood of errors or that improve program predictability by defining behavior in the presence of errors.

5.1   OPTIONAL PARTS OF THE SYNTAX

Parts of the Ada syntax, while optional, can enhance the readability of the code. The
guidelines given below concern use of some of these optional features.

5.1.1   Loop Names

guideline

- Associate names with loops when they are nested ([6] page 195).

example

```
...
DOCUMENT_PAGES:
   loop
      ...
      PAGE_LINES:
         loop
            ...
            exit PAGE_LINES when LINE_NUMBER = MAX_LINES_ON_PAGE;
            ...
            LINE_SYMBOLS:
               loop
                  ...
                  exit LINE_SYMBOLS when CURRENT_SYMBOL = SENTINEL;
                  ...
               end LINE_SYMBOLS;
            ...
         end PAGE_LINES;
      ...
      exit DOCUMENT_PAGES when PAGE_NUMBER = MAXIMUM_PAGES;
      ...
   end DOCUMENT_PAGES;
...
```

rationale

When you associate a name with a loop, you <u>must</u> include that name with the
associated end for that loop [28]. This helps readers find the associated end for
any given loop. This is especially true if loops are broken over screen or page
boundaries. The choice of a good name for the loop documents its purpose,
reducing the need for explanatory comments. If a name for a loop is very difficult
to choose, this could indicate a need for more thought about the algorithm.

Regularly naming loops will also help you follow Guideline 5.1.3.

It can be difficult to think up a name for every loop, therefore the guideline
specifies nested loops. The benefits in readability and second thought outweigh
the inconvenience of naming the loops.

5.1.2   Block Names

guideline

- Associate names with blocks when they are nested.

example

```
TRIP:
   declare
      -- local object declarations
   begin
      ARRIVE_AT_AIRPORT:
         declare
            -- local object declarations
         begin
            -- Activities to RENT_CAR,
            -- Activities to CLAIM_BAGGAGE,
            -- Activities to RESERVE_HOTEL.
            -- Exception handlers, etc.
         end ARRIVE_AT_AIRPORT;

      VISIT_CUSTOMER:
         declare
            -- local object declarations
         begin
            -- again a set of activities...
            -- exception handlers, etc.
         end VISIT_CUSTOMER;

      DEPARTURE_PREPARATION:
         declare
            -- local object declarations
         begin
            -- Activities to RETURN_CAR,
            -- Activities to CHECK_BAGGAGE,
            -- Activities to WAIT_FOR_FLIGHT.
            -- Exception handlers, etc.
         end DEPARTURE_PREPARATION;

      BOARD_RETURN_FLIGHT;
   end TRIP;
```

rationale

When there is a nested block structure it can be difficult to determine to which block a given end corresponds.   Naming blocks alleviates this confusion.   The choice of a good name for the block documents its purpose, reducing the need for explanatory comments.   If a name for the block is very difficult to choose, this could indicate a need for more thought about the algorithm.

This guideline is also useful if nested blocks will be broken over a screen or page boundary.

It can be difficult to think up a name for each block, therefore the guideline specifies nested blocks. The benefits in readability and second thought outweigh the inconvenience of naming the blocks.

5.1.3   Exit Statements

guideline

- Use loop names on exit statements from nested loops.

example

See the example in Section 5.1.1.

rationale

When there is a nested loop structure and an exit statement is used, it can be difficult to determine which loop is being exited. Naming loops and their exits alleviates this confusion.

This guideline is also useful if nested loops will be broken over a screen or page boundary.

5.1.4   Naming End Statements

guideline

- Include the simple name at the ends of a package specification and body.

- Include the simple name at the ends of a task specification and body.

- Include the simple name at the end of an accept statement.

- Include the designator at the end of a subprogram body.

example

```
--------------------------------------------------------------------
package AUTOPILOT is
   ...
   function IS_ENGAGED ... ;
   ...
   procedure DISENGAGE ... ;
   ...
end AUTOPILOT;
--------------------------------------------------------------------
package body AUTOPILOT is
--------------------------------------------------------------------
   task type COURSE_MONITOR is
      ...
      entry RESET ... ;
      ...
   end COURSE_MONITOR;
--------------------------------------------------------------------
   function IS_ENGAGED ... is
      ...
   end IS_ENGAGED;
--------------------------------------------------------------------
   procedure DISENGAGE ... is
      ...
   end DISENGAGE;
--------------------------------------------------------------------
   task body COURSE_MONITOR is
      ...
      accept RESET ... do
         ...
      end RESET;
      ...
   end COURSE_MONITOR;
--------------------------------------------------------------------
end AUTOPILOT;
--------------------------------------------------------------------
```

rationale

The ends of compound statements include indicators of what they end. Repeating names on the ends of these units ensures consistency throughout the code. In addition, the named end provides a reference for the reader if the unit spans a page or screen boundary, or if it contains a nested unit.

5.2 PARAMETER LISTS

A subprogram or entry parameter list is the interface to the abstraction implemented by the subprogram or entry. As such, it is important that it is clear, and is expressed in a consistent style. Careful decisions about formal parameter naming and ordering can make the purpose of the subprogram easier to understand, and easier to use when its purpose is understood. While not strictly an interface issue in the same sense as the above, similar considerations apply to the use of aggregates.

5.2.1   Formal Parameters

guideline

- Name formal parameters so as to obviate the need for comments describing their purpose.

example

```
procedure ASSEMBLE_TELEMETRY_MESSAGE
    (INPUT_PACKET                : in      TELEMETRY_PACKET;
     TRANSFER_TO_DOWNLINK_BUFFER : in out PACKET_BUFFER;
     BUFFER_FULL                 :     out BOOLEAN);
```

rationale

Formal parameters are local to a routine. As with local variables, their names should fully express their purpose. Following the variable naming guidelines (3.3.1 and 3.3.3) for formal parameters will make the code within the body read more like natural language, and thus be self documenting. In choosing parameter names, keep in mind that the code may be viewed by an audience that is uninitiated in the problem domain (e.g., signal processing). Conversely, the code may be viewed by an audience that is fluent in the problem domain and uninitiated in software development.

5.2.2   Named Association ‡

guideline

- Use named parameter association in calls of infrequently used subprograms or entries with many formal parameters.

- Use named component association for constants, expressions, and literals in aggregate initializations.

- Use named association when instantiating generics with many formal parameters.

- Use named association for clarification when the actual parameter is TRUE or FALSE or an expression.

- Use named association when supplying a non-default value to an optional parameter.

example

```
ENCODE_TELEMETRY_PACKET
  (SOURCE          => POWER_ELECTRONICS;
   CONTENT         => TEMPERATURE;
   VALUE           => READ_TEMPERATURE_SENSOR(POWER_ELECTRONICS);
   TIME            => CURRENT_TIME;
   SEQUENCE        => NEXT_PACKET_ID;
   VEHICLE         => THIS_SPACECRAFT;
   PRIMARY_MODULE  => TRUE);
```

rationale

Calls of infrequently used subprograms or entries with many formal parameters can be difficult to understand without referring to the subprogram or entry code. Named parameter association can make these calls more readable.

When the formal parameters have been named appropriately, it is easy to determine exactly what purpose the subprogram serves without looking at its code. This reduces the need for named constants that exist solely to make calls more readable. It also allows variables used as actual parameters to be given names indicating what they are without regard to why they are being passed in a call. An actual parameter which is an expression rather than a variable cannot be named otherwise.

note

The judgment of when named parameter association will improve readability is essentially subjective. Certainly, extremely simple or familiar subprograms such as a two element swap routine or a sine function do not require the extra clarification of named association in the procedure call. You might consider any subprogram or entry with four or more parameters as a candidate for named parameter association.

caution

A consequence of named parameter association is that the formal parameter names may not be changed without modifying the text of each call.

5.2.3   Default Parameters

guideline

- Provide default parameters to allow for occasional special usage of widely used subprograms or entries.
- Place default parameters at the end of the formal parameter list.
- Consider default parameters when expanding functionality.

example

Chapter 14 of the Ada LRM [28] contains many superb examples of this practice.

rationale

Often, the vast majority of uses of a subprogram or entry will need the same value for a given parameter. Providing that value as the default for the parameter will make the parameter optional on the majority of calls. It will also allow the remaining calls to customize the subprogram or entry by providing different values for that parameter.

Placing default parameters at the end of the formal parameter list allows the caller to use positional association on the call, otherwise defaults are available only when named association is used.

Often during maintenance activities, you will increase the functionality of a subprogram or entry. This will require more parameters than the original form for some calls. Provide new parameters to control this new functionality. Give the new parameters default values which specify the old functionality. Calls needing the old functionality need not be changed as they will take the defaults. New calls needing the new functionality can specify that by providing other values for the new parameters.

This enhances maintainability in that the places which use the modified routines do not themselves have to be modified, while the previous functionality levels of the routines are allowed to be "reused."

exceptions

Do not go overboard. If the changes in functionality are truly radical, you should be preparing a separate routine rather than modifying an existing one. One indicator of this situation would be that it is difficult to determine value combinations for the defaults that uniquely and naturally require the more restrictive of the two functions. In such cases it is better to go ahead with creation of a separate routine.

5.2.4   Mode Indication

guideline

- Show the mode indication of procedure and entry parameters [18].

example

```
procedure OPEN_FILE (FILE_NAME    : in    SPC_STRING;
                     OPEN_STATUS :      out STATUS_CODES);

entry      ACQUIRE    (KEY         : in    CAPABILITY;
                       RESOURCE    :      out TAPE_DRIVE);
```

rationale

By showing the mode of parameters you aid the reader. If you do not specify a parameter mode, the default mode is in. Explicitly showing the mode indication of all parameters is a more assertive action than simply taking the default mode. Anyone reviewing the code at a later date will be more confident that you intended the parameter mode to be in.

5.2.5 Order of Parameter Declarations ‡

guideline

- Declare parameters in a consistent order [25].

example

In this example, the chosen order is all in parameters, followed by all in out parameters, followed by all out parameters.

```
procedure ASSEMBLE_TELEMETRY_MESSAGE
    (INPUT_PACKET                 : in      TELEMETRY_PACKET;
     TRANSFER_TO_DOWNLINK_BUFFER  : in out  PACKET_BUFFER;
     BUFFER_FULL                  :     out BOOLEAN);
```

rationale

By declaring all the parameters in a consistent order, you make the code easier to read and understand. Some of your choices are to arrange the parameters by in, in out, and out, or to group the parameters by function. In any case, all default parameters must be at the end of the parameter list.

note

In special cases, parameters declared in a non-standard order may be more readable. Since consistency is the goal, however, the readability or some other quality of the code must be enhanced if you deviate from this guideline. Default parameters are an example of the need for a special case.

5.3 TYPES

In addition to determining the possible values for variables, type names and distinctions can be very valuable aids in developing safe, readable, and understandable code. Types clarify the structure of your data and can limit or restrict the operations that can be performed on that data. "Keeping types distinct has been found to be a very powerful means of detecting logical mistakes when a program is written and to give valuable assistance whenever the program is being subsequently maintained" [20]. Take advantage of Ada's strong typing capability in the form of subtypes, derived types, task types, private types and limited private types.

The guidelines encourage much code to be written to ensure strong typing (i.e., subtypes). While it might appear that there would be execution penalties for this amount of code, this is usually not the case. In contrast to other conventional languages, Ada has a less direct relationship between the amount of code that is written and the size of the resulting executable program. Most of the strong type checking is performed at compilation time rather than execution time, so the size of the executable code is not greatly affected.

5.3.1 Derived Types and Subtypes

guideline

- Use existing types as building blocks by deriving new types from them.
- Use range constraints on subtypes to help make the compiler's constraint checking beneficial.
- Define new types, especially derived types, to include the largest set of possible values, including boundary values.
- Constrain the ranges of derived types with subtypes, excluding boundary values.

example

Type TABLE is a building block for creation of new types:

```
type TABLE is
   record
      COUNT : LIST_SIZE  := EMPTY;
      LIST  : ENTRY_LIST := EMPTY_LIST;
   end record;

type TELEPHONE_DIRECTORY  is new TABLE;
type DEPARTMENT_INVENTORY is new TABLE;
```

The following are distinct types that cannot be intermixed in operations not programmed explicitly to use them both:

```
type DOLLARS is new NUMBER;
type CENTS   is new NUMBER;
```

Below, SOURCE_TAIL has a value outside the range of LISTING_PAPER when the line is empty. All the indices can be mixed in expressions, as long as the results fall within the correct subtypes:

```
type      COLUMNS         is range FIRST_COLUMN - 1 .. LISTING_WIDTH + 1;
subtype LISTING_PAPER     is COLUMNS
                             range FIRST_COLUMN     .. LISTING_WIDTH;
subtype DUMB_TERMINAL     is COLUMNS
                             range FIRST_COLUMN     .. DUMB_TERMINAL_WIDTH;

type      LISTING_LINE    is array(LISTING_PAPER) of BYTES;
type      TERMINAL_LINE   is array(DUMB_TERMINAL) of BYTES;

SOURCE_TAIL               : COLUMNS       := COLUMNS´FIRST;
SOURCE                    : LISTING_LINE;
DESTINATION               : TERMINAL_LINE;
...
DESTINATION(DESTINATION´FIRST .. (SOURCE_TAIL - DESTINATION´LAST)) :=
    SOURCE(COLUMNS´SUCC(DESTINATION´LAST) .. SOURCE_TAIL);
```

rationale

The name of a derived type can make clear its intended use and avoid proliferation of similar type definitions. Objects of two derived types, even though derived from the same type, cannot be mixed in operations unless such operations are supplied explicitly or one is converted to the other explicitly. This prohibition is an enforcement of strong typing.

Define new types, derived types and subtypes cautiously and deliberately. The concepts of subtype and derived type are not equivalent, but they can be used to advantage in concert. A subtype limits the range of possible values for a type. It does not define a new type.

Types can have highly constrained sets of values without eliminating useful values. Used in concert, derived types and subtypes can eliminate many flag variables and type conversions within executable statements. This renders the program more readable while allowing the compiler to enforce strong typing constraints.

This combination of derived types and subtypes allows use of sentinel values. It allows compatibility between subtypes within subexpressions without type conversions (in C, this is called a type cast) everywhere as would happen with derived types alone.

Many algorithms begin or end with values just outside the normal range. If boundary values are not compatible within subexpressions, algorithms can be needlessly complicated. The program can become cluttered with flag variables and special cases when it could just test for zero or some other sentinel value.

note

The price of the reduction in the number of independent type declarations is that any types derived from some base type are dependent on both the range of, and the subprograms derived from, the base type and are subject to change without warning when the base type is redefined. This trickle-down of changes is sometimes a blessing and sometimes a curse.

5.3.2   Anonymous Types

guideline

- Do not use anonymous types.

example

```
-- use
type BUFFER is array (BUFFER_INDEX) of CHARACTER;
INPUT_LINE : BUFFER;
-- rather than
INPUT_LINE : array (BUFFER_INDEX) of CHARACTER;
```

Warning! INPUT_LINE and OUTPUT_LINE below are of different types!

```
INPUT_LINE, OUTPUT_LINE : array (BUFFER_INDEX) of CHARACTER;
```

rationale

Although Ada allows anonymous types, they have limited usefulness and complicate program modification. For example, a variable of anonymous type can never be used as an actual parameter because the type of the formal parameter will be different. Even though this may not be a limitation initially, it precludes a modification in which a piece of code is changed to a procedure.

note

For task types, see Guideline 6.1.2. For unconstrained arrays as formal parameters, see Guideline 8.3.9.

You will notice, in reading the Ada LRM [28], that there are cases when anonymous types are mentioned abstractly as part of the description of the Ada computational model. These cases do not violate this guideline.

5.3.3   Private Types

guideline

- Use limited private types in preference to private types.
- Use private types in preference to non-private types.
- Explicitly export needed operations rather than easing restrictions.

example

```
-----------------------------------------------------------------------
package PACKET_TELEMETRY is
   type FRAME_HEADER is limited private;
   type FRAME_DATA is private;
   type FRAME_CODES is (
      MAIN_BUS_VOLTAGE, TRANSMITTER_1_POWER,
      ...
   );
   ...
-----------------------------------------------------------------------
private
   type FRAME_HEADER is
      record
         ...;
      end record;

   type FRAME_DATA is
      record
         ...
      end record;
   ...
end PACKET_TELEMETRY;
-----------------------------------------------------------------------
```

rationale

Limited private types and private types support abstraction and information hiding better than non-private types. The more restricted the type, the better information hiding is served. The ripple effect of changes is thus lessened. The structure of a non-private type is exposed to the package's users, so any operation that would be available had the user declared the type himself is available for that type.

The more restricted the operations you allow on the types a package exports, the more information about the package's implementation is hidden from its users. This, in turn, allows the implementation to change without affecting the rest of the program, and it protects the implementation of the package from corruption by misuse. While there are many valid reasons to use exported types, it is better to try the preferred route first, loosening the restrictions only as necessary. If it is necessary for a user of the package to use a few of the restricted operations, it is better to export the operations explicitly and individually via exported subprograms than to drop a level of restriction. This practice retains the restrictions on other operations.

Limited private types have the most restricted set of operations available to users of a package. Of the types that must be made available to users of a package, as many as possible should be limited private. The operations available to limited private types are membership tests, selected components, components for the selections of any discriminant, qualification and explicit conversion, and attributes

'BASE and 'SIZE. Objects of a limited private type have attributes 'ADDRESS, 'SIZE, and, if there are discriminants, 'CONSTRAINED. None of these operations allow the user of the package to manipulate objects in a way that depends on the structure of the type.

If additional operations must be available to the type, the restrictions may be loosened by making it a private type. The operations available on objects of private types that are not available on objects of limited private types are assignment and tests for equality and inequality.

5.4 DATA STRUCTURES

The data structuring capabilities of Ada are a powerful resource, therefore use them to model the data as closely as possible. It is possible to group logically related data and let the language control the abstraction and operations on the data rather than requiring the programmer or maintainer do so. Data can also be organized in a building block fashion. In addition to showing how a data structure is organized (and possibly giving the reader an indication as to why it was organized that way), creating the data structure from smaller components allows those components to be reused themselves. Using the features that Ada provides can increase the maintainability of your code.

5.4.1 Heterogeneous Data

guideline

- Use records to group heterogeneous but related data.

example

```
type PROPULSION_METHOD is ( SAIL, DIESEL, NUCLEAR );
type CRAFT is
    record
        NAME   : STRING ( ... );
        PLANT  : PROPULSION_METHOD;
        LENGTH : FEET;
        BEAM   : FEET;
        DRAFT  : FEET;
    end record;
type FLEET is array ( ... ) of CRAFT;
```

rationale

By gathering related data into the same construct, you help the maintainer find all of it, simplifying any modifications that apply to all rather than part. This in turn increases reliability. Neither you nor an unknown maintainer are liable to forget to deal with all the pieces of information in the executable statements.

The idea is to put the information a maintainer needs to know where it can be found with the minimum of effort. If, as in the example, all information relating to a given CRAFT is in the same place, the relationship is clear both in the declarations and especially in the code accessing and updating that information. But if it is scattered among several data structures, it is less obvious that this is an intended relationship as opposed to a coincidental one. In the latter case, the declarations may be grouped together to imply intent, but it may not be possible to group the accessing and updating code that way. Ensuring the use of the same index to access the corresponding element in each of several parallel arrays is difficult if the accesses are at all scattered.

note

It may seem desirable to store heterogeneous data in parallel arrays in what amounts to a FORTRAN–like style. This style is an artifact of FORTRAN's data structuring limitations. FORTRAN only has facilities for constructing homogeneous arrays. Ada's record types offer one way to specify what are called non–homogeneous arrays or heterogeneous arrays. If you are new to languages of this nature, you may need to remind yourself occasionally of the opportunity afforded by Ada to group related data.

exceptions

If you run into any one of the following scenarios, a different organization of your data would be required:

- If the application must interface directly to hardware, the use of complex data structures could be confusing and get in the way, or it may not map onto the layout of the hardware in question.

- If the application must interface to foreign code, do not use structures any more complicated than those that the foreign code supports. This will simplify the interfacing process.

- If there are efficiency concerns about the overhead incurred for heterogeneous data structures, group the data using comments in order to illustrate the design. First, determine whether the concerns are well–founded.

As always, if the guideline must be violated, document what you did, and why.

5.4.2   Nested Records

guideline

- Record structures should not always be flat. Factor out common parts.

- For a large record structure, group related components into smaller subrecords.

- Declare subrecords separately.

- For nested records, pick element names that will read well when inner elements are referenced.

example

```
type COORDINATE is
   record
      ROW    : LOCAL_FLOAT;
      COLUMN : LOCAL_FLOAT;
   end record;

type WINDOW is
   record
      TOP_LEFT     : COORDINATE;
      BOTTOM_RIGHT : COORDINATE;
   end record;
```

rationale

You can make complex data structures understandable and comprehensible by composing them of familiar building blocks. This technique works especially well for large record types with parts which fall into natural groupings. The components factored into separately declared records based on a common quality or purpose correspond to a lower level of abstraction than that represented by the larger record.

note

A carefully chosen name for the component of the larger record that will be used to select the smaller enhances readability, e.g.,

"`if WINDOW1.BOTTOM_RIGHT.ROW > WINDOW2.TOP_LEFT.ROW then . . .`"

caution

Everything can be taken to extremes, so be wary. Do not break a structure up into so many fragments that it becomes difficult to understand. Be careful not to nest compound structures too deeply (e.g., arrays of records of arrays ...). Be especially wary of discriminated records whose defaults require large amounts of storage. The multiplication of space required by objects builds rapidly as structures are nested. You may be taking up a good-sized portion of available memory without realizing it.

5.4.3   Dynamic Data

guideline

- Differentiate between static and dynamic data. Use dynamically allocated objects with caution.

- Use dynamically allocated data structures only when it is necessary to create and destroy them dynamically or to be able to reference them by different names.

- Do not drop pointers.
- Do not create dangling references.
- Initialize all access variables and components.
- Do not rely on any properties of a garbage collector.
- Deallocate explicitly.
- Use length clauses.
- Provide handlers for STORAGE_ERROR.

example

These lines show how a dangling reference might be created:

```
P1 := new OBJECT;
P2 := P1;
UNCHECKED_OBJECT_DEALLOCATION(P2);
```

This line can raise an exception due to referencing the deallocated object:

```
X := P1.DATA;
```

In the following three lines, if there is no intervening assignment of P1's value to any other pointer, the object created on the first line is no longer accessible after the third line.

```
P1 := new OBJECT
    ...
P1 := P2;
```

rationale

See also Guidelines 5.9.1, 5.9.2 and 6.1.3 for variations on these problems. A dynamically allocated object is an object created by the execution of an allocator. Allocated objects referenced by access variables allow you to generate *aliases,* multiple references to the same object. Anomalous behavior can arise when you reference a deallocated object by another name. This is called a *dangling reference.* Totally disassociating a still-valid object from all names is called *dropping a pointer.* A dynamically allocated object that is not associated with a name cannot be deallocated explicitly or referenced.

A dropped pointer depends on an asynchronous garbage collector for reclamation of space. It also raises questions in the mind of the reader as to whether the loss of access to the object was intended or a mistake.

An implementation is not required to provide a garbage collector at all, so of course you cannot depend on one's properties. Using the unchecked deallocation facility permits use of an incremental garbage collector rather than depending on an asynchronous one. It also documents a deliberate decision to abandon the object. A method of ensuring space reclamation is to implement an incremental garbage collector of your own. This is normally called a free list. Any implementation-provided garbage collector can be disabled with pragma CONTROLLED.

Uninitialized access variables are essentially dangling references. Any uninitialized, or un-reset, component of a record or array can also be a dangling reference or carry a bit pattern representing inconsistent data. The dangers of dangling references are that you may attempt to use them, thereby overwriting reallocated space, or reading data that was intended to be inaccessible. As a result, any additional information you may try to store in it can be overwritten asynchronously or, worse, you may overwrite information needed by the garbage-collection and memory-allocation systems.

Whenever you use dynamic allocation, it is possible to run out of space. Ada provides a facility (a length clause) for requesting the size of the pool of allocation space at compile time. Anticipate that you can still run out at run time. Prepare handlers for the exception STORAGE_ERROR, and consider carefully what alternatives you may be able to include in the program for each such situation.

There is a school of thought that dictates avoidance of all dynamic allocation. It is largely based on fear of the occurrence which in Ada raises STORAGE_ERROR. Facilities such as length clauses and handlers for exception STORAGE_ERROR make this fear unfounded. The situation is little different than allocating elements of an array in FORTRAN. In Ada, much of the accounting is done for you.

5.5   EXPRESSIONS

Properly coded expressions can enhance the readability and understandability of a program. Poorly coded expressions can turn a program into a maintainer's nightmare.

5.5.1   Range Values

guideline

- Use 'FIRST and 'LAST instead of numeric literals to represent the first and last values of a range.

- Use only 'FIRST and 'LAST to represent the first and last indices of arrays.

- Use 'RANGE wherever you can.

example

```
type TEMPERATURE      is ALL_TIME_LOW .. ALL_TIME_HIGH;
type WEATHER_STATIONS is 1 .. MAX_STATIONS;
WEATHER_DATA : array (WEATHER_STATIONS) of TEMPERATURE;
...
WEATHER_DATA(WEATHER_STATIONS'FIRST) := TEMPERATURE'LAST;
```

rationale

Ada provides attributes for many predefined and user–defined types. Using them eliminates dependence on an underlying implementation such as the bounds of an array or the range of a subtype. This enhances program reliability.

caution

An example in ([12] page 12) shows an error where the ´RANGE attribute was used on the type INTEGER rather than on a constrained (array) type. Be careful that you associate attributes with the proper types and subtypes.

5.5.2   Array Attributes

guideline

- Use array attributes ´FIRST, ´LAST, ´LENGTH, or ´RANGE instead of numeric literals for accessing arrays.

example

```
subtype NAME_STRING_SIZE is POSITIVE range 1.. 30;
NAME_STRING : STRING (NAME_STRING_SIZE);

for I in NAME_STRING´RANGE loop
  <sequence of statements>
end loop;
```

rationale

When you use attributes, the declared array size can be changed without affecting code that depends on its ´RANGE.

Ada provides many attributes for predefined and user–defined types. Using them eliminates dependence on an underlying implementation such as the bounds of an array or the range of a subtype. This enhances program reliability.

5.5.3   Parenthesized Expressions

guideline

- Use parentheses to specify the order of subexpression evaluation where operators from different precedence levels are involved, and to clarify expressions [16] [17].

example

```
(1.5 * (X**2)) + (6.5 * X) + 47
```

rationale

Parenthesizing expressions improves code readability. For cases where one might forget which operator has higher precedence, it may be helpful to use parentheses to specify the order of subexpression evaluation.

5.5.4 Positive Forms of Logic

guideline

- Avoid names and constructs that rely on the use of negatives.

- Choose names of flags so they represent states that can be used in positive form.

example

```
-- Use
if OPERATOR_MISSING
-- rather than either
if not OPERATOR_FOUND
-- or
if not OPERATOR_MISSING
```

Both of the following improvements switch to positive forms and help follow Guideline 5.6.4:

```
-- Use
loop
   exit when END_OF_FILE;
-- rather than
while not END_OF_FILE loop
```

```
-- Use
loop
   exit when CURRENT_CHARACTER = SENTINEL;
-- rather than
while CURRENT_CHARACTER /= SENTINEL loop
```

rationale

Relational expressions can be more readable and understandable when stated in a positive form. As an aid in choosing the name, consider that the most frequently used branch in a conditional construct should be encountered first.

exception

There are cases in which the negative form is unavoidable. If the relational expression better reflects what is going on in the code, then inverting the test to adhere to this guideline is not recommended.

5.5.5 Short Circuit Forms of the Logical Operators

guideline

- Use short−circuit forms of the logical operators.

example

```
-- Use
if not (Y = 0) or else (X / Y /= 10) ...
-- rather than either
if (Y /= 0) and (X / Y = 10) ...
-- or
if (X / Y = 10) ...
-- to avoid NUMERIC_ERROR.

-- Use
if TARGET /= null and then TARGET.DISTANCE < THRESHOLD then ...
-- rather than
if TARGET.DISTANCE < THRESHOLD then ...
-- to avoid referencing a field in a non-existent object.
```

rationale

The use of short−circuit control forms prevents a class of data−dependent errors or exceptions that can occur as a result of expression evaluation. The short−circuit forms guarantee an order of evaluation and an exit from the sequence of relational expressions as soon as the expression's result can be determined.

In the absence of short−circuit forms, Ada does not provide a guarantee of the order of expression evaluation, nor does the language guarantee that evaluation of a relational expression is abandoned when it becomes clear that it will evaluate to FALSE.

note

If it is important that all parts of a given expression be evaluated, the expression probably violates Guideline 4.1.3 which prohibits side−effects in functions.

5.5.6 Type Qualified Expressions and Type Conversions

guideline

- Use type qualified expressions instead of type conversions wherever possible.

example

```
type REAL is ...
type WHOLE is ...

ACTUAL_SPEED  : REAL;
DESIRED_SPEED : WHOLE; -- Console dial setting
TAIL_WIND     : WHOLE; -- Cheap sensor

ACTUAL_SPEED := REAL(DESIRED_SPEED + TAIL_WIND);
-- A type conversion. An addition operation inherited by subtype WHOLE is
--  used, followed by conversion of the result to REAL

ACTUAL_SPEED := REAL'(DESIRED_SPEED + TAIL_WIND);
-- A type qualified expression. A specific operator overloading + and
--  giving result type REAL is used.
```

rationale

Type qualified expressions are evaluated at compile time, but type conversions are made at execution time. Type qualifiers help in operator overload resolution by explicitly specifying the qualified expressions' desired result type.

5.5.7   Accuracy of Operations with Real Operands

guideline

- Use "<=" and ">=" in relational expressions with real operands instead of "=".

example

```
CURRENT_TEMPERATURE   : TEMPERATURE := 0.0;
TEMPERATURE_INCREMENT : TEMPERATURE := 1.0 / 3.0;
MAXIMUM_TEMPERATURE   : constant     := 100.0;

...
loop
    ...
    CURRENT_TEMPERATURE := CURRENT_TEMPERATURE + TEMPERATURE_INCREMENT;
    ...
    exit when CURRENT_TEMPERATURE >= MAXIMUM_TEMPERATURE;
    ...
end loop;
```

rationale

Fixed and floating point values, even if derived from similar expressions, may not be exactly equal. The imprecise, finite representations of real numbers in hardware always have round-off errors so that any variation in the construction path or history of two reals has the potential for resulting in different numbers even when the paths or histories are mathematically equivalent.

The Ada definition of model intervals also means that the use of <= is more transportable than either < or =.

note

Floating point arithmetic is treated in Chapter 7.

exceptions

If your application must test for an exact value of a real number (e.g. testing the precision of the arithmetic on a certain machine), then the "=" would have to be used. But never use "=" on real operands as a condition to exit a loop.

5.6 STATEMENTS

Careless or convoluted use of statements can make a program hard to read and maintain even if its global structure is well organized. You should strive for simple and consistent use of statements to achieve clarity of local program structure. Some of the guidelines in this section counsel use or avoidance of particular statements. As is pointed out in the individual guidelines, rigid adherence to those guidelines would be excessive, but experience has shown that they generally lead to code with improved reliability and maintainability.

5.6.1 Nesting ‡

guideline

- Restrict or minimize the depth of nested expressions and control structures [18].

- Try simplification heuristics.

rationale

Deeply nested structures are confusing, difficult to understand, and difficult to maintain. The problem lies in the difficulty of determining what part of a program is contained at any given level. For expressions, this is important in achieving the correct placement of balanced grouping symbols and in achieving the desired operator precedence. For control structures, the question involves what part is controlled. Specifically, is a given statement at the proper level of nesting, i.e., is it too deeply or too shallowly nested, or is the given statement associated with the proper choice, e.g. for if or case statements? Indentation helps, but it is not a panacea. Visually inspecting alignment of indented code (mainly intermediate levels) is an uncertain job at best. In order to minimize the complexity of the code, keep the maximum number of nesting levels to between three and five.

note

Asking yourself this list of questions can help you consider alternatives to the code and sometimes help you reduce the nesting:

– Does some part of the expression or the lower nested control structures represent a significant, and perhaps reusable computation that I can factor into a subprogram?

– Can I convert these nested if statements into a case statement?

– Am I using `else if` where I could be using `elsif`?

– Can I re–order the conditional expressions controlling this nested structure?

– Is there a different design that would be simpler?

exceptions

If nesting must be used to ensure proper scope and visibility that cannot be attained by using subprograms, then proceed cautiously and take especial care with the choice of identifiers and loop and block names. If deep nesting is required frequently, there may be overall design decisions for the code that should be changed.

Some algorithms require deeply nested loops and segments controlled by conditional branches. Their continued use can be ascribed to their efficiency and time proven utility.

5.6.2   Slices

guideline

• Use slices rather than a loop to copy all or part of an array.

example

```
type SQUARE_MATRIX    is array (ROWS, ROWS) of ELEMENT;
type DIAGONALS        is array (1 .. 3)     of ELEMENT;
type ROW_VECTOR       is array (ROWS)       of ELEMENT;
type TRI_DIAGONAL     is array (ROWS)       of DIAGONALS;
MARKOV_PROBABILITIES :    SQUARE_MATRIX;
TEMPORARY_VECTOR     :    ROW_VECTOR;
DIAGONAL_DATA        :    TRI_DIAGONAL;
...
-- Simple slice assignment.
TEMPORARY_VECTOR := MARKOV_PROBABILITIES( 1 );
...
-- Remove diagonal and off-diagonal elements.
DIAGONAL_DATA(ROWS'FIRST)( 1 )    := NULL_VALUE;
DIAGONAL_DATA(ROWS'FIRST)(2 .. 3) :=
  MARKOV_PROBABILITIES(ROWS'FIRST)(ROWS'FIRST .. ROWS'SUCC(ROWS'FIRST));

for I in ROWS'SUCC(ROWS'FIRST) .. ROWS'PRED(ROWS'LAST) loop
   DIAGONAL_DATA( I ) := MARKOV_PROBABILITIES( I )(I - 1 .. I + 1);
end loop;

DIAGONAL_DATA(ROWS'LAST)(1 .. 2) :=
  MARKOV_PROBABILITIES(ROWS'LAST)(ROWS'PRED(ROWS'LAST) .. ROWS'LAST);
DIAGONAL_DATA(ROWS'LAST)( 3 )    := NULL_VALUE;
```

rationale

An assignment statement with slices is simpler and clearer than a loop, and helps the reader see the intended action. Slice assignment can be faster than a loop if a block move instruction is available.

5.6.3   Case Statements

guideline

- Always use an others choice on case statements

- Enumerate all possibilities, eliding over ranges.

- If you intend a possibility to be handled in an others choice, comment that choice out and mark it with "OTHERS" (see example).

- If you use an if statement instead of a case statement, use marker comments indicating the cases, and use a trailing else part for the others choice.

- Bias use of the others choice toward error detection.

example

```
-- (In procedure RECOGNIZE_SYMBOLS)
case CURRENT_CHARACTER is
   ...
   when '0' .. '9' => SCAN_NUMERIC_LITERAL;
   when ':'        => DISCERN_COLON_COLON_EQUAL;
   ...
   when 'A' .. 'Z' => SCAN_IDENTIFIER;
-- when '['        => -- OTHERS
-- when '\'        => -- OTHERS
   ...
   when 'a' .. 'z' => SCAN_IDENTIFIER;
   ...
   when others     => raise ILLEGAL_SOURCE_CHARACTER;
end case;
```

rationale

Absence of an others choice when you have not enumerated all possibilities leaves you open to raising an exception should the omitted possibility arise. The statement that "it can never happen" is unacceptable programming practice. You must assume it can happen and be in control when it occurs. You should provide defensive code routines for the "cannot get here" conditions.

A compiler will not complain about an others choice when you have enumerated all possibilities. Commenting a possibility out shows that you did not forget that case and points to its being handled in the others choice.

A case statement can be more efficient than a nested if-then-else structure. Where the case statement is less efficient, marking the if statement documents the intended purpose and allows the if to be converted back to a case should the code move to a different implementation or machine.

Because the others choice is a catch–all for possibilities you have not enumerated, it is better to treat those possibilities as errors than to risk performing an unintended action for a possibility you simply forgot to list above.

5.6.4 Loops

guideline

- Use for loops wherever possible.
- Use plain loops with exit statements where for loops are not appropriate.
- Avoid use of a while iteration scheme.

example

Situations requiring a "loop and a half" arise often. For this use:

```
loop
   P;
   exit when CONDITION_DEPENDENT_ON_P;
   Q;
end loop;
```

rather than:

```
P;
while not CONDITION_DEPENDENT_ON_P loop
   Q;
   P;
end loop;
```

rationale

A for loop is bounded, so it cannot be an "infinite loop." There is a certainty of understanding for the reader and the writer not associated with other forms of loops. The thought and care given to the iteration range is often greater than that given to other forms of loops. Properly coded, the iteration range can change automatically and correctly whenever the data structures upon which the loop body operates change.

The Ada Rationale [27] points out that the plain loop with exit statements is the preferred looping structure for the language, and that the while construct was only added as a special case to comfort former Pascal programmers. Once you are used to seeing the plain loop with exit's, the exit statement no longer seems to "hide" in the loop body.

The loop with exit statements is necessary to provide the semantics associated with the Pascal repeat..until. It also supports loops which must terminate somewhere within the sequence of statements of the body; that is, to provide for a "loop and a half" construct. Complicated "loop and a half" constructs simulated with while constructs often require the introduction of flag variables, making programs more complex and less reliable.

Most people are better able to think in terms of stopping conditions than of continuation conditions. An exit statement and its placement are explicit indicators of the termination condition. A while loop requires inverted logic in the control expression. The inverted logic of trying to express a continuation condition often leads to negative forms violating Guideline 5.5.4.

As a result, the continuation condition in the while construct is often confused with the loop invariant. If the condition programmed into the while condition happens to be the loop invariant, the loop is guaranteed to be infinite. One way to prevent this is to avoid the while construct. Guideline 5.6.6 discusses another way to prevent infinite loops.

The problem of forgetting to include an exit statement can be easily solved by having a static analyzer warn of such loops. A warning does not preclude a loop intended to be infinite; rather, it highlights it.

Use of several exit statements within a loop does not decrease the provability of a program. Cristian [10] has shown that proof of multi–exit control structures is no more difficult than proof of single–exit control structures.

exceptions

There are a few occasions when expressing a continuation condition is so much more natural than expressing a stopping condition that it is reasonable to use the while loop.

5.6.5   Exit Statements

guideline

- Use exit statements to enhance the readability of loop termination code [17].

- Use "`if ... then ... exit`" only to express "last wishes" [17].

- Review exit statement placement.

example

See the examples in Guidelines 5.1.1 and 5.6.4.

rationale

It is more readable to use exit statements than to try to add boolean flags to a while loop condition to simulate exits from the middle of a loop. Even if all exit statements would be clustered at the top of the loop body, the separation of a complex condition into multiple exit statements can simplify and make it more readable and clear. The sequential execution of two exit statements is often more clear than the short-circuit control forms.

The form "`if <condition> then <statements> exit; end if;`" allows some statements to be executed only on that exit path yet before that path rejoins any other exit paths following the loop body. Such statements are termed "last wishes." This is an important capability, but it has the disadvantage of lowering the exit statement to a deeper nesting level. Where there is no need for last wishes, the form "`exit when <condition>`" is much more readable.

Loops with many scattered exit statements can be indicative of fuzzy thinking as regards the loop's purpose in the algorithm. Such an algorithm might be coded better some other way, e.g., with a series of loops. Some rework can often reduce the number of exit statements and make the code clearer.

See also Guidelines 5.1.3 and 5.6.4.

5.6.6   Safe Programming

guideline

- <u>Understand</u> and consider specifying bounds on loops.

- <u>Understand</u> and consider specifying bounds on recursion.

example

Establishing an iteration bound:

```
SAFETY_COUNTER := 0;
PROCESS_LIST:
   loop
      exit when CURRENT_ITEM = null;
      ...
      CURRENT_ITEM := CURRENT_ITEM.NEXT;
      ...
      SAFETY_COUNTER := SAFETY_COUNTER + 1;
      if SAFETY_COUNTER > 1_000_000 then
         raise SAFETY_ERROR;
      end if;
   end loop PROCESS_LIST;
```

Establishing a recursion bound:

```
---------------------------------------------------------------------
procedure DEPTH_FIRST(ROOT            : in SUBTREE;
                      ...
                      SAFETY_COUNTER : in RECURSION_BOUND := 1_000) is
begin
   if SAFETY_COUNTER = 0 then
      raise RECURSION_ERROR;
   end if;
   ... -- normal subprogram body
   DEPTH_FIRST(SUB_ROOT, ..., (SAFETY_COUNTER - 1)); -- recursive call
   ...
end DEPTH_FIRST;
---------------------------------------------------------------------
```

Using the subprogram. One call specifies a maximum recursion depth of 50. The second takes the default (one thousand). The third uses a computed bound:

```
DEPTH_FIRST(TREE, ..., 50);
DEPTH_FIRST(TREE, ... );
DEPTH_FIRST(TREE, ..., CURRENT_TREE_HEIGHT);
```

rationale

Recursion, and iteration using structures other than for statements, can be infinite because the expected terminating condition does not arise. Such faults are sometimes quite subtle, may occur rarely, and may be difficult to detect because an external manifestation might be absent or substantially delayed.

By including, in addition to the loops themselves, counters and checks on the counter values you can prevent many forms of infinite loop. The inclusion of such checks is one aspect of the technique called Safe Programming [2].

The bounds of these checks do not have to be exact, just realistic. Such counters and checks are not part of the primary control structure of the program but a benign addition functioning as an execution–time "safety net" allowing error detection and possibly recovery from potential infinite loops or infinite recursion.

Including specific bounds can save considerable effort during program development and maintenance. Once the loop is understood, very little effort is required to insert the bounds check, especially if a syntax–directed editor is used.

note

If a loop uses the for iteration scheme (Guideline 5.6.4), it follows this guideline.

exceptions

Embedded control applications will have loops that are intended to be infinite. Only a few loops within such applications should qualify as exceptions to this guideline. The exceptions should be deliberate (and documented) policy decisions.

In general, violation of this guideline is only appropriate for trivial loops where the termination criteria have been proven, at least informally.

5.6.7   Goto Statements

guideline

- Do not use goto statements unless you are sure there is no alternative.

- If you must use a goto statement, highlight both it and the label.

rationale

A goto statement is an unstructured change in the control flow. Worse, the label does not require an indicator of where the corresponding goto statement(s) are. This makes code unreadable and makes its correct execution suspect.

note

For the rare occasions in which you can present a case for using a goto statement, highlight both it and the label with blank space and highlighting comments, and indicate at the label where the corresponding goto statement(s) may be found.

5.6.8   Return Statements

guideline

- Minimize the number of returns from a subprogram [17].

- Highlight returns with comments or white space to keep them from being lost in other code.

rationale

Excessive use of returns can make code confusing and unreadable. Only use returns where warranted. Too many returns from a subprogram may be an indicator of cluttered logic. If the application requires multiple returns, use them at the same level (i.e., as in different branches of a case statement), rather than scattered throughout the subprogram code. Some rework can often reduce the number to one and make the code more clear.

exception

Do not avoid return statements if it detracts from natural structure and code readability.

5.6.9   Blocks

guideline

- Use blocks cautiously and for their intended purposes.

- Do not use blocks to place subprograms in-line "by hand."

example

```
...
INTEGRATE_VELOCITY_FROM_ACCELERATION:
   begin
      ...
   exception
      when NUMERIC_ERROR | CONSTRAINT_ERROR =>
         ... -- use old velocity value
   end INTEGRATE_VELOCITY_FROM_ACCELERATION;
...
```

rationale

The intended purposes of blocks are to introduce local declarations, to define local exception handlers, and to perform local renaming. One category included in local declarations is, of course, tasks.

Local renaming reduces the length of qualified pathnames where there would be no confusion. In this sense, it is analogous to the Pascal with statement.

Using abstraction in the form of subprogram calls generally enhances readability and understandability. When performance is an issue, the pragma INLINE can be used.

5.7 VISIBILITY

As noted in Section 4.2, Ada's ability to enforce information hiding and separation of concerns through its visibility controlling features is one of the most important advantages of the language, particularly when "programming–in–the–large" where a team of programmers are producing a large system. Subverting these features, for example by over liberal use of the use clause, is wasteful and dangerous.

5.7.1 The Use Clause

guideline

- Minimize use of the use clause [18].
- Localize the effect of the use clauses you must employ.

example

This is a modification of the example from Guideline 4.2.3. The effect of a use clause is localized.

```
---------------------------------------------------------------------------
procedure COMPILER is
---------------------------------------------------------------------------
   package LISTING_FACILITIES is

      procedure NEW_PAGE_OF_LISTING;
      procedure NEW_LINE_OF_PRINT;
      -- etc.

   end LISTING_FACILITIES;
---------------------------------------------------------------------------
   package body LISTING_FACILITIES  is separate;
---------------------------------------------------------------------------
begin --COMPILER
   ...
end COMPILER;
---------------------------------------------------------------------------
```

```
with TEXT_IO;
   separate (COMPILER)
package body LISTING_FACILITIES is
   ------------------------------------------------------------------
   procedure NEW_PAGE_OF_LISTING is
   begin
      ...
   end NEW_PAGE_OF_LISTING;
   ------------------------------------------------------------------
   procedure NEW_LINE_OF_PRINT is
      use TEXT_IO;                                    -- Note use clause.
   begin
      ...
   end NEW_LINE_OF_PRINT;
   ------------------------------------------------------------------
   -- etc

end LISTING_FACILITIES;
   ------------------------------------------------------------------
```

rationale

Avoiding the use clause forces you to use fully qualified names. In large systems, there may be many library units named in a with clause. When a corresponding use clause accompanies the with clause, and the simple names of the library packages are omitted (as is allowed by the use clause), references to external entities will be obscured, and identification of external dependencies becomes difficult.

You can minimize the scope of the use clause by placing it in the body of a package or subprogram, or encapsulating it in a block to restrict visibility. Placing a use clause in a block has a similar effect to the Pascal with statement of localizing the use of unqualified names.

notes

Avoiding the use clause completely can cause problems when compiling with (in the context of) packages that contain type declarations. Simply importing these types via a with clause does not allow relational operators implicitly defined for them to be used in infix notation. A use clause enables the use of infix notation. You can use renaming declarations to overcome the visibility problem and enable the use of infix notation.

Avoiding the use clause completely also causes problems with enumeration literals. They must be fully qualified as well. Unfortunately, you cannot conveniently overcome this problem by renaming declarations.

An argument defending the use clause can be found in [21].

5.7.2   The Renames Clause

guideline

- Use the renames clause judiciously and purposefully.

- Rename a long fully qualified name to reduce the complexity if it becomes unwieldy (Guideline 3.1.4).

- Rename declarations for visibility purposes rather than using the use clause (Guideline 5.7.1).

- Rename parts when interfacing to reusable components originally written with inapplicable nomenclature.

example

```
procedure DISK_WRITE (TRACK_NAME : TRACK; ITEM : DATA) renames
   SYSTEM_SPECIFIC.DEVICE_DRIVERS.DISK_HEAD_SCHEDULER.TRANSMIT;
```

rationale

If the renaming facility is abused, it can be difficult for readers of the code. A renames clause can substitute an abbreviation for a qualifier or long package name locally. This can make code more readable yet anchor the code to the full name. However, the use of renames clauses can often be avoided or made obviously undesirable by choosing names with such care that fully qualified names read well. The list of renaming declarations serves as a list of abbreviation definitions (see Guideline 3.1.4). By renaming imported infix operators, the use clause can often be avoided. The method prescribed in the Ada LRM [28] for renaming a type is to use a subtype (see Guideline 3.4.1). Often the parts recalled from a reuse library will not have names that are as general as they could be or that match the new application's naming scheme. An interface package exporting the renamed subprograms can map to your project's nomenclature.

5.7.3   Overloaded Subprograms

guideline

- Limit the use of overloading to widely used subprograms that perform similar actions on arguments of different types [18].

example

```
function SIN (ANGLES : MATRIX_OF_RADIANS) return MATRIX;
function SIN (ANGLES : VECTOR_OF_RADIANS) return VECTOR;
function SIN (ANGLE  : RADIANS          ) return SMALL_REAL;
function SIN (ANGLE  : DEGREES          ) return SMALL_REAL;
```

rationale

Excessive overloading can be confusing to maintainers ([18] page 65). Only use it when there is overwhelming reason to do so. There is also the danger of hiding declarations if overloading becomes habitual.

note

This guideline does not necessarily prohibit subprograms with identical names declared in different packages.

5.7.4 Overloaded Operators

guideline

- Preserve the conventional meaning of overloaded operators [18].

- Use "+" to identify adding, joining, increasing, and enhancing kinds of functions.

- Use "-" to identify subtraction, separation, decreasing, and depleting kinds of functions.

example

```
function "+" (X : MATRIX:
              Y : MATRIX) return MATRIX;

...

SUM_MATRIX := MATRIX_A + MATRIX_B;
```

rationale

Subverting the conventional interpretation of operators leads to confusing code.

note

There are potential problems with any overloading. For example, if there are several versions of the "+" operator, and a change to one of them affects the number or order of its parameters, locating the occurrences that must be changed can be difficult.

5.8 USING EXCEPTIONS

Ada exceptions are a reliability–enhancing language feature designed to help specify program behavior in the presence of errors or unexpected events. Exceptions are not intended to provide a general purpose control construct. Further, liberal use of exceptions should not be considered sufficient for providing full software fault tolerance [15].

5.8.1   Disasters versus State Information

guideline

- Use the exception mechanism for abnormal or extremely unusual occurrences only.

- Use exceptions to enhance readability by separating fault handling from normal execution.

- Treat all exceptions as disasters.

- Do not use exceptions to return normal state information. Use parameters as flags instead.

rationale

Normal and predictable events should be handled by the code without the asynchronous transfer of control represented by an exception.

When fault handling and only fault handling code is included in exception handlers, the reader of your code can concentrate on the normal processing algorithm or on the fault handling code as the need arises. This removes the burden of continually determining, for each set of statements, into which category they fall.

With the above separation, an exception represents a very unusual and undesirable event, a disaster. The very fact that the flow of control cannot return from the handler to the point at which the exception was raised indicates the intent that desperate measures are required to deal with the situation.

The semantics of exceptions, with a complete change in execution path, makes it difficult to associate the point of a call with all of the points in the calling frame where execution could continue. This situation is intolerable for returning (status) information which is expected from the usual call. Code to discriminate among cases presented by status information should be placed near the call to which it pertains.

5.8.2   User-, Implementation-, and Predefined Exceptions

guideline

- Declare user-defined exceptions for use in explicit raise statements.

- Do not explicitly raise predefined or implementation-defined exceptions.

- Catch and convert or handle all predefined and implementation-defined exceptions at the earliest opportunity.

example

```
-- Use
raise POSITION_IS_ZERO;   -- User defined, signaling misuse of abstraction.
-- rather than either
raise NUMERIC_ERROR;      -- This is a misuse of a predefined exception.
-- or
raise CONSTRAINT_ERROR;   -- This is a misuse of a predefined exception.
```

rationale

User–defined exception names can be made more descriptive in a particular situation than the predefined exception names. In addition, there are already too many situations that result in the predefined exceptions. Creating additional causes for predefined exceptions increases the difficulty of determining the source of an exception. An exception name should have one, and not several, meanings. Raising, say, CONSTRAINT_ERROR in an abstract data type implementation may seem consistent with the interface presented by the predefined types, but this actually obscures meaning and, in this case, makes programming (of exception handlers) more difficult than it would be otherwise.

Implementation–defined exceptions are non–portable and have meanings which are subject to change even between successive compiler releases. This introduces too much uncertainty for the creation of useful handlers.

Converting an exception means raising a user–defined exception in the handler for the original exception. This introduces a meaningful name for export to the user of the frame. It is more informative for the reader and the writer of the code calling the frame, since it raises the abstraction level of the error situation above that of the hardware and language combination. Once the error situation is couched in terms of the application, it can be handled in those terms.

5.8.3   Handlers for others

guideline

- Provide a handler for others in suitable frames to protect against unexpected exceptions being propagated without bound.

- Use others only to catch exceptions you cannot enumerate explicitly, preferably only to flag a potential abort.

- Use caution when programming handlers for others.

- Avoid using others during development.

rationale

Providing a handler for others allows you to follow the other guidelines in this section. It affords a place to catch and convert truly unexpected exceptions that were not caught by the explicit handlers. It may be possible to provide "fire walls" against unexpected exception being propagated without providing handles in every frame. By placing an others handler in every frame, however, you can convert the unexpected exceptions as soon as they are raised. The others handler cannot discriminate between different exceptions, and, as a result, any such handler must treat the exception as a disaster. Even such a disaster can still be converted into an abstraction–related user–defined exception at that point. Since a handler for others will catch any exception not otherwise handled explicitly, one placed in the frame of a task or of the main subprogram affords the opportunity to perform final clean–up and to shut down cleanly.

Failing to enumerate all known exceptions and leaving it up to the handler for others to deal with them all is shirking your duties.

Programming a handler for others requires caution because it cannot discriminate either which exception was actually raised or precisely where it was raised. Thus the handler cannot make any assumptions about what can be or even what needs to be "fixed."

The use of handlers for others during development, when exception occurrences can be expected to be frequent, can hinder debugging. It is much more informative to the developer to see a traceback with the actual exception listed than the converted exception. Furthermore, many tracebacks will not list the point where the original exception was raised once it has been caught by a handler.

note

The arguments in the preceding paragraph apply only to development time, when traceback listings are useful. They are not useful to users, and can be dangerous. The handler should be included in comment form at the outset of development and the double dash removed before delivery.

5.8.4   Propagation

guideline

- Handle all exceptions, both user and predefined.
- For every exception that might be raised, provide a handler in suitable frames to protect against undesired propagation outside the abstraction.

rationale

The statement that "it can never happen" is not an acceptable programming approach. You must assume it can happen and be in control when it occurs. You should provide defensive code routines for the "cannot get here" conditions.

Some extant advice calls for catching and propagating any exception to the calling unit. That advice will stop a program. What you should do is catch the exception and propagate it, or a substitute (see Guideline 5.8.2), only if your handler is at the wrong abstraction level to effect recovery. Effecting recovery can be difficult, but the alternative is a program that does not meet its specification.

Making an explicit request for termination implies that your code is in control of the situation and has determined that to be the only safe course of action. Being in control affords opportunities to shut down in a controlled manner (clean up loose ends, close files, release surfaces to manual control, sound alarms), and implies that all available programmed attempts at recovery have been made.

5.8.5   Localizing the Cause of an Exception

guideline

- Do not rely on being able to identify the fault raising predefined or implementation-defined exceptions.

- Use blocks to associate localized sections of code with their own exception handlers.

example

See Guideline 5.6.9.

rationale

It is very difficult to determine in an exception handler exactly which statement and which operation within that statement raised an exception, particularly the predefined and implementation-defined exceptions. The predefined and implementation-defined exceptions are candidates for conversion and propagation to higher abstraction levels for handling there. User-defined exceptions, being more closely associated with the application, are better candidates for recovery within handlers.

User-defined exceptions can also be difficult to localize. Associating handlers with small blocks of code helps to narrow the possibilities, making it easier to program recovery actions. The placement of handlers in small blocks within a subprogram or task body also allows resumption of the subprogram or task after the recovery actions. If you do not handle exceptions within blocks, the only action available to the handlers is to shut down the task or subprogram as prescribed in Guideline 5.8.4.

note

The optimal size for the sections of code you choose to protect by a block and its exception handlers is very application-dependent. Too small a granularity forces you to expend much more effort in programming for abnormal actions than for the normal algorithm. Too large a granularity reintroduces the problems of determining what went wrong and of resuming normal flow.

5.9   ERRONEOUS EXECUTION

An Ada program is *erroneous* when it violates or extends the rules of the language governing program behavior. Neither compilers nor run–time environments are able to detect erroneous behavior in all circumstances and contexts. In many cases the normal function of the hardware violates no Ada rules, but adds additional constraints.   In these cases, the erroneous Ada program is correct for the implementation. The effects of erroneous execution are unpredictable ([28] §1.6). If the compiler does detect an instance of an erroneous program, its options are to indicate a compile time error, to insert the code to raise PROGRAM_ERROR, and possibly to write a message to that effect, or to do nothing at all.

Erroneousness is not a concept unique to Ada. The guidelines below describe or explain the specific instances of erroneousness defined in the Ada LRM [28].

5.9.1   Unchecked Conversion

guideline

- Use UNCHECKED_CONVERSION only with utmost care ([28] §13.10.2).

rationale

An unchecked conversion is a bit–for–bit copy without regard to the meanings attached to those bits and bit positions by either the source or the destination type. The source bit pattern can easily be meaningless in the context of the destination type. Unchecked conversions can create values that will violate type constraints on subsequent operations. Unchecked conversion of objects mismatched in size has implementation-dependent results.

5.9.2   Unchecked Deallocation

guideline

- Use UNCHECKED_DEALLOCATION with caution.

rationale

Most of the reasons for using unchecked deallocation with caution have been given in Guideline 5.4.3. When this feature is used, there is no checking that there is only one access path to the storage being deallocated. Thus, any other access paths are not made null. Depending on such a check is erroneous.

This feature has its place. When using an implementation that does not have an asynchronous garbage collector, it may be better to use unchecked deallocation than simply to "drop pointers" whenever a dynamically allocated object becomes useless. This at least has the potential for freeing some space for reallocation.

5.9.3   Dependence on Parameter Passing Mechanism

guideline

- Do not write code whose correct execution depends on the parameter passing mechanism used by an implementation [28] [8].

example

The output of this program depends on the particular parameter passing mechanism that was used.

```
-------------------------------------------------------------------------
with TEXT_IO;
use  TEXT_IO;
procedure OUTER is
   type COORDINATES is
      record
         X : INTEGER := 0;
         Y : INTEGER := 0;
      end record;

   OUTER_POINT : COORDINATES;

   package INTEGER_IO is new TEXT_IO.INTEGER_IO(INTEGER);
   use INTEGER_IO;
-------------------------------------------------------------------------
   procedure INNER (INNER_POINT : in out COORDINATES) is
   begin -- INNER
      INNER_POINT.X := 5;

      -- The following line causes the output of the program to
      -- depend on the parameter passing mechanism.
      PUT(OUTER_POINT.X);
   end INNER;
-------------------------------------------------------------------------
begin -- OUTER
   PUT(OUTER_POINT.X);
   INNER(OUTER_POINT);
   PUT(OUTER_POINT.X);
end OUTER;
-------------------------------------------------------------------------
```

If the parameter passing mechanism is by copy, the results on the standard output file will be:
0 0 5

If the parameter passing mechanism is by reference, the results will be:
0 5 5

rationale

The language definition specifies that a parameter whose type is array, record or task type can be passed by copy or by reference. It is erroneous to assume that either mechanism is used in a particular case.

exceptions

Frequently, when interfacing Ada to foreign code, dependence on parameter passing mechanisms used by a particular implementation is unavoidable. In this case, isolate the calls to the foreign code in an interface package that exports operations that do not depend on the parameter-passing mechanism.

5.9.4   Multiple Address Clauses

guideline

- Use address clauses to map variables and entries to the hardware device or memory, not to model the FORTRAN "equivalence" feature.

example

```
SINGLE_ADDRESS : CONSTANT := ...
...

INTERRUPT_VECTOR_TABLE : HARDWARE_ARRAY;
    for INTERRUPT_VECTOR_TABLE use at SINGLE_ADDRESS;
```

rationale

The result of specifying a single address for multiple objects or program units is undefined, as is specifying multiple addresses for a single object or program unit. Specifying multiple address clauses for an interrupt entry is also undefined. It does not necessarily overlay objects or program units, or associate a single interrupt with more than one task entry.

5.9.5   Suppression of Exception Check

guideline

- Do not suppress exception checks during development.
- Minimize suppression of exception checks during operation.

rationale

If you disable exception checks and program execution results in a condition in which an exception would otherwise occur, the program execution is erroneous. The results are unpredictable. Further, you must still be prepared to deal with the suppressed exceptions if they are raised in and propagated from the bodies of subprograms, tasks, and packages you call.

The pragma SUPPRESS grants an implementation permission to suppress runtime checks, it does not require it to do so. It cannot be relied upon as a general technique for performance improvement.

If you need to use pragma SUPPRESS, postpone it until it is clear that the program is correct, but too slow, and there is no other alternative for improving performance. Pragma SUPPRESS can then be used to improve performance for specific, well–understood objects/types.

5.9.6   Initialization

guideline

- Initialize all objects prior to use.

- Ensure elaboration of an entity before using it.

- Do not use function calls in declarations.

example

```
-----------------------------------------------------------------------
package ROBOT_CONTROLLER is
    ...
    function SENSE return POSITION;
    ...
end ROBOT_CONTROLLER;
-----------------------------------------------------------------------
package body ROBOT_CONTROLLER is
    ...
    GOAL : POSITION := SENSE;
                    --------                    The underlined text is illegal.
    ...
-----------------------------------------------------------------------
    function SENSE return POSITION is
        ...
    end SENSE;
-----------------------------------------------------------------------
begin -- ROBOT_CONTROLLER
    GOAL := SENSE;                      -- This line is legal.
    ...
end ROBOT_CONTROLLER;
-----------------------------------------------------------------------
```

rationale

Ada does not define an initial default value for objects of any type other than access types. Using the value of an object before it has been assigned a value will raise an exception or result in erroneous program execution. Objects can be initialized implicitly by declaration or explicitly by assignment statements. Initialization at the point of declaration is safest as well as easiest for maintainers. You can also specify default values for fields of records as part of the type declarations for those records.

An unelaborated function called within a declaration (initialization) raises an exception that must be handled outside of the unit containing the declarations. This is true for any exception the function raises even if it has been elaborated.

Ensuring initialization does not imply initialization at the declaration. In the example, GOAL must be initialized via a function call. This cannot occur at the declaration, but can occur as part of the sequence of statements of the body of the enclosing package.

note

Sometimes, elaboration order can be dictated with pragma ELABORATE. Pragma ELABORATE only applies to library units.

5.10 SUMMARY

optional parts of the syntax

- Associate names with loops when they are nested.

- Associate names with blocks when they are nested.

- Use loop names on exit statements from nested loops.

- Include the simple name at the ends of a package specification and body.

- Include the simple name at the ends of a task specification and body.

- Include the simple name at the end of an accept statement.

- Include the designator at the end of a subprogram body.

parameter lists

- Name formal parameters so as to obviate the need for comments describing their purpose.

- Use named parameter association in calls of infrequently used subprograms or entries with many formal parameters.

- Use named component association for constants, expressions, and literals in aggregate initializations.

- Use named association when instantiating generics with many formal parameters.

- Use named association for clarification when the actual parameter is TRUE or FALSE or an expression.

- Use named association when supplying a non-default value to an optional parameter.

- Provide default parameters to allow for occasional special usage of widely used subprograms or entries.

- Place default parameters at the end of the formal parameter list.
- Consider default parameters when expanding functionality.
- Show the mode indication of procedure and entry parameters.
- Declare parameters in a consistent order.

types

- Use existing types as building blocks by deriving new types from them.
- Use range constraints on subtypes to help make the compiler's constraint checking beneficial.
- Define new types, especially derived types, to include the largest set of possible values, including boundary values.
- Constrain the ranges of derived types with subtypes, excluding boundary values.
- Do not use anonymous types.
- Use limited private types in preference to private types.
- Use private types in preference to non-private types.
- Explicitly export needed operations rather than easing restrictions.

data structures

- Use records to group heterogeneous but related data.
- Record structures should not always be flat. Factor common parts.
- For a large record structure, group related components into smaller subrecords.
- Declare subrecords separately.
- For nested records, pick element names that will read well when inner elements are referenced.
- Differentiate between static and dynamic data. Use dynamically allocated objects with caution.
- Use dynamically allocated data structures only when it is necessary to create and destroy them dynamically or to be able to reference them by different names.
- Do not drop pointers.
- Do not create dangling references.
- Initialize all access variables and components.
- Do not rely on any properties of a garbage collector.

- Deallocate explicitly.
- Use length clauses.
- Provide handlers for STORAGE_ERROR.

expressions

- Use ´FIRST and ´LAST instead of numeric literals to represent the first and last values of a range.
- Use only ´FIRST and ´LAST to represent the first and last indices of arrays.
- Use ´RANGE wherever you can.
- Use array attributes ´FIRST, ´LAST, ´LENGTH, or ´RANGE instead of numeric literals for accessing arrays.
- Use parentheses to specify the order of subexpression evaluation where operators from different precedence levels are involved, and to clarify expressions.
- Avoid names and constructs that rely on the use of negatives.
- Choose names of flags so they represent states that can be used in positive form.
- Use short–circuit forms of the logical operators.
- Use type qualified expressions instead of type conversions wherever possible.
- Use "<=" and ">=" in relational expressions with real operands instead of "=".

statements

- Restrict or minimize the depth of nested expressions and control structures.
- Try simplification heuristics.
- Use slices rather than a loop to copy all or part of an array.
- Always use an others choice on case statements
- Enumerate all possibilities, eliding over ranges.
- If you intend a possibility to be handled in an others choice, comment that choice out and mark it with "OTHERS".
- If you use an if statement instead of a case statement, use marker comments indicating the cases, and use a trailing else part for the others choice.
- Bias use of the others choice toward error detection.
- Use for loops wherever possible.
- Use plain loops with exit statements where for loops are not appropriate.

- Avoid use of a while iteration scheme.
- Use exit statements to enhance the readability of loop termination code.
- Use "if ... then ... exit" only to express "last wishes".
- Review exit statement placement.
- <u>Understand</u> and consider specifying bounds on loops.
- <u>Understand</u> and consider specifying bounds on recursion.
- Do not use goto statements unless you are sure there is no alternative.
- If you must use a goto statement, highlight both it and the label.
- Minimize the number of returns from a subprogram.
- Highlight returns with comments or white space to keep them from being lost in other code.
- Use blocks cautiously and for their intended purposes.
- Do not use blocks to place subprograms in-line "by hand".

visibility

- Minimize use of the use clause.
- Localize the effect of the use clauses you must employ.
- Use the renames clause judiciously and purposefully.
- Rename a long fully qualified name to reduce the complexity if it becomes unwieldy.
- Rename declarations for visibility purposes rather than using the use clause.
- Rename parts when interfacing to reusable components originally written with inapplicable nomenclature.
- Limit the use of overloading to widely used subprograms that perform similar actions on arguments of different types.
- Preserve the conventional meaning of overloaded operators.
- Use "+" to identify adding, joining, increasing, and enhancing kinds of functions.
- Use "-" to identify subtraction, separation, decreasing, and depleting kinds of functions.

using exceptions

- Use the exception mechanism for abnormal or extremely unusual occurrences only.

- Use exceptions to enhance readability by separating fault handling from normal execution.

- Treat all exceptions as disasters.

- Do not use exceptions to return normal state information. Use parameters as flags.

- Declare user–defined exceptions for use in explicit raise statements.

- Do not explicitly raise predefined or implementation–defined exceptions.

- Catch and convert or handle all predefined and implementation–defined exceptions at the earliest opportunity.

- Provide a handler for others in suitable frames to protect against unexpected exceptions being propagated without bound.

- Use others only to catch exceptions you cannot enumerate explicitly, preferably only to flag a potential abort.

- Use caution when programming handlers for others.

- Avoid using others during development.

- Handle all exceptions, both user and predefined.

- For every exception that might be raised, provide a handler in suitable frames to protect against undesired propagation outside the abstraction.

- Do not rely on being able to identify the fault raising predefined or implementation–defined exceptions.

- Use blocks to associate localized sections of code with their own exception handlers.

erroneous execution

- Use UNCHECKED_CONVERSION only with utmost care.

- Use UNCHECKED_DEALLOCATION with caution.

- Do not write code whose correct execution depends on the parameter passing mechanism used by an implementation.

- Use address clauses to map variables and entries to the hardware device or memory, not to model the FORTRAN "equivalence" feature.

- Do not suppress exception checks during development.

- Minimize suppression of exception checks during operation.

- Initialize all objects prior to use.

- Ensure elaboration of an entity before using it.

- Do not use function calls in declarations.

Chapter 6

Concurrency

Concurrent programming is difficult and error prone. The concurrent programming features of Ada are designed to make it easier to write and maintain concurrent programs which behave consistently and predictably, and avoid such problems as deadlock and starvation. The language features themselves cannot guarantee that programs will have these desirable properties; they must be used with discipline and care, a process supported by the guidelines in this chapter.

A pitfall to be avoided at all costs is the misuse of language features, for example using priorities for synchronization, because of the presumed inefficiency of the proper Ada construct (in this case, the rendezvous). Bear in mind that a program that does the wrong thing, however fast, is incorrect, and that such misuses can be particularly dangerous because the program may behave correctly some of the time (for example, during testing).

Another pitfall is to assume that the rules of good sequential program design can be applied, by analogy, to concurrent programs. For example, while multiple returns from subprograms should be discouraged (Guideline 5.6.8), multiple task exits or termination points are often necessary and desirable.

6.1 TASKING

Tasks provide a means, within the Ada language, of expressing concurrent, asynchronous, threads of control, enabling some properties of concurrent programs to be checked at compile time and to be independent of the idiosyncrasies of a particular operating system. However, to capitalize on the potential advantages of tasks it is important to use tasks for their intended purposes, and with a clear understanding of their semantics and the semantics of their associated language features.

6.1.1   Tasks

guideline

- Use tasks to model abstract, asynchronous entities within the problem domain.
- Use tasks to control or synchronize access to tasks or other asynchronous entities (e.g., asynchronous I/O, peripheral devices, interrupts).
- Use tasks to define concurrent algorithms.
- Use tasks to perform cyclic or prioritized activities [17].

rationale

These are the intended uses of tasks. They all revolve around the fact that a task has its own thread of control separate from the main subprogram. The conceptual model for a task is that it is a program with its own virtual processor. This provides the opportunity to model entities from the problem domain in terms more closely resembling those entities, and the opportunity to deal with physical devices on their own terms as a separate concern from the main algorithm of the application. Tasks also allow the programming of naturally concurrent activities in their own terms, and they can be mapped to multiple processors when these are available.

6.1.2   Task Types

guideline

- Do not use anonymous task types.
- Differentiate between static and dynamic tasks [17] [18].

example

The example illustrates the syntactic differences between the kinds of tasks discussed here. BUFFER is static and has a name, but its type is anonymous. Because it is declared explicitly, the task type BUFFER_MANAGER is not anonymous. CHANNEL is static and has a name, and its type is not anonymous. Like all dynamic objects, ENCRYPTED_PACKET_QUEUE.ALL is essentially anonymous, but its type is not.

```
task BUFFER is ...
task type BUFFER_MANAGER is ...
type REPLACEABLE_BUFFER is access BUFFER_MANAGER;
ENCRYPTED_PACKET_QUEUE : POINTER_TO_TASK;
CHANNEL : BUFFER_MANAGER;
...
ENCRYPTED_PACKET_QUEUE := new BUFFER_MANAGER;
```

rationale

The consistent and logical use of task types when necessary contributes to understandability.

The use of named tasks of anonymous type would avoid a proliferation of task types that were only used once, and the practice does communicate to maintainers that there are no other task objects of that type. However, a program originally written using named tasks that must be enhanced to contain several tasks of the same type will require more work to upgrade than the same program written with task types. The extra work involves including task type declarations and deciding whether static or dynamic tasks should be used.

Guideline 7.3.2 requires the use of task types because a task storage representation clause can be applied to a task type, but not to a task object.

Identical tasks can be derived from a common task type. Dynamically allocated task structures are necessary when you must create and destroy tasks dynamically or when you must reference them by different names.

6.1.3   Dynamic Tasks

guideline

- Use caution with dynamically allocated task objects.

- Avoid referencing terminated tasks through their aliases.

- Avoid disassociating a task from all names.

example

In this example, the limited number of trackable radar targets are tasks continuously updating their positions based on previous position and velocity until corrected by a new scan. Out-of-range targets are dropped (through use of the abort statement). There are bugs in the design.

Let these lines in subprograms in the radar package be executed first:

```
TARGET(LATEST_ACQUISITION) := new RADAR_TRACK;
TARGET(LATEST_ACQUISITION).INITIALIZE
   (SELF     =>           TARGET(LATEST_ACQUISITION),
    VELOCITY => ...                                     ,
    POSITION => ...                             );
 ...
```

Let these lines in the body of task type RADAR_TRACK execute next. They are not inside an accept statement:

```
...
NEW_POSITION := INTEGRATE(POSITION, VELOCITY);
if OUT_OF_RANGE(NEW_POSITION) then
   abort SELF; --notice abort
...
```

Let this line in a subprogram in the radar package execute third. This line can raise TASKING_ERROR due to calling an entry of an aborted task:

```
TARGET(SCAN_HIT).CORRECT_READINGS(POSITION,VELOCITY);
```

rationale

A dynamically allocated task object is a task object created by the execution of an allocator. Allocated task objects referenced by access variables allow you to generate *aliases;* multiple references to the same object. Anomalous behavior can arise when you reference an aborted task by another name. The example illustrates an attempt to call an entry in an aborted task after the abort operation was applied to the alias.

A dynamically allocated task that is not associated with a name (a "dropped pointer") cannot be referenced for the purpose of making entry calls, nor can it be the direct target of an abort statement (see Guideline 5.4.3).

6.1.4 Priorities

guideline

- Do not use the pragma PRIORITY to handle synchronization [18].

example

At some point in its execution, T1 is blocked. Otherwise, we would not expect T2 or SERVER to ever get anything done. If T1 is blocked, it is possible for T2 to reach its call to SERVER's entry (OPERATION) before T1. Suppose this has happened and that T1 now makes its entry call before SERVER has a chance to accept T2's call.

```
task T1 ... PRIORITY HIGH    ... SERVER.OPERATION ...
task T2 ... PRIORITY MEDIUM  ... SERVER.OPERATION ...
task SERVER                  ... accept OPERATION ...
```

This is the timeline of events so far:

```
T1 blocks
T2 calls SERVER.OPERATION
T1 unblocks
T1 calls SERVER.OPERATION
SERVER accepts the call from T1 or from T2?
```

Some people might expect that, due to its higher priority, T1's call would be accepted by SERVER before that of T2. The synchronization between T1 and SERVER is not affected (and certainly not effected) by T1's priority. This is called *priority inversion*.

rationale

The pragma PRIORITY is only intended to be used to determine relative importance of tasks with respect to one another. Entry calls are queued in FIFO order, not priority order. This can lead to a situation called priority inversion, where lower priority tasks are given service while higher priority tasks remain blocked.

A program like the one in the example might behave many times as expected. You cannot rely on it continuing to do so, as that behavior would be due more to happenstance than to the programmed priorities. Task priorities are even less reliable as a means of achieving mutual exclusion.

6.1.5   Delay Statements

guideline

- Do not depend on a particular delay being achievable [18].

- Never use a busy waiting loop instead of a delay.

- Design to limit polling to those cases where absolutely necessary.

- Never use knowledge of the execution pattern of tasks to achieve timing requirements.

example

```
NO_DRIFT:
   declare
      use CALENDAR;
      -- INTERVAL is a global constant of type DURATION
      NEXT_TIME : TIME := CLOCK + INTERVAL;
   begin
      PERIODIC:
         loop
            delay NEXT_TIME - CLOCK;
            ... -- some actions
            NEXT_TIME := NEXT_TIME + INTERVAL;
         end loop PERIODIC;
   end NO_DRIFT;
```

rationale

The Ada language definition only guarantees that the delay time is a minimum. The meaning of a delay statement is that the task will not be scheduled for execution before the interval has expired. There is no guarantee of when (or if!) it will be scheduled after the interval. This must be the case in light of the potentially ever-changing task and priority mix with which the scheduling algorithm must deal.

A busy wait can only interfere with processing by other tasks. It can consume the very processor resource necessary for completion of the activity for which it is waiting. Even a loop with a delay can be seen as busy waiting if the wait is significantly longer then the delay interval. If a task has nothing to do, it should be blocked at an accept or select statement.

Prevention of drift in a periodic activity can be achieved by calculating the next time–to–occur based on the actual time of the current execution. The example illustrates this tactic, but note that this tactic does not handle jitter.

Using knowledge of the execution pattern of tasks to achieve timing requirements is non–portable since the underlying scheduling algorithm may change.

6.2   COMMUNICATION

The need for tasks to communicate gives rise to most of the problems that make concurrent programming so difficult. Used properly, Ada's inter–task communication features can improve the reliability of concurrent programs; used thoughtlessly they can introduce subtle errors that can be difficult to detect and correct.

6.2.1   Defensive Task Communication

guideline

- Provide a handler for exception PROGRAM_ERROR wherever there is no else part in a selective wait statement [25].

- Make systematic use of handlers for TASKING_ERROR.

- Be prepared to handle exceptions during a rendezvous.

example

This block allows recovery from exceptions raised while attempting to communicate a command to a task controlling the throttle.

```
ACCELERATE:
    begin
        THROTTLE.INCREASE(STEP);
    exception
        when TASKING_ERROR =>
            ...
        when CONSTRAINT_ERROR
            | NUMERIC_ERROR =>
            ...
        when THROTTLE_TOO_WIDE =>
            ...
        ...
    end ACCELERATE;
```

In this select statement, if all the guards happen to be closed, the program can continue by executing the else part. There is no need for a handler for PROGRAM_ERROR. Other exceptions can still be raised while evaluating the guards or attempting to communicate.

```
BUFFER:
   begin
      select
         when ... =>
            accept ...
      or
         when ... =>
            accept ...
      else
         ...
      end select;
   exception
      when CONSTRAINT_ERROR
         | NUMERIC_ERROR =>
         ...
   ...
   end BUFFER;
```

In this select statement, if all the guards happen to be closed, exception
PROGRAM_ERROR will be raised. Other exceptions can still be raised while evaluating
the guards or attempting to communicate.

```
BUFFER:
   begin
      select
         when ... =>
            accept ...
      or
         when ... =>
            delay ...
      end select;
   exception
      when PROGRAM_ERROR =>
         ...
      when CONSTRAINT_ERROR
         | NUMERIC_ERROR =>
         ...
   ...
   end BUFFER;
```

rationale

The exception PROGRAM_ERROR is raised if a selective wait statement is reached, all
of whose alternatives are closed (i.e., the guards evaluate FALSE), unless there is
an else part. When all alternatives are closed, the task can never again progress,
so there is by definition an error in its programming. You must be prepared to
handle this error should it occur.

Since an else part cannot have a guard, it can never be closed off as an alternative
action, thus its presence prevents PROGRAM_ERROR. Recall, however, that an else
part, a delay alternative, and a terminate alternative are all mutually exclusive, so
you will not always be able to provide an else part. In these cases, you must be
prepared to handle PROGRAM_ERROR.

The exception TASKING_ERROR can be raised in the calling task whenever it attempts to communicate. There are many situations permitting this. Few of them are preventable by the calling task.

If an exception is raised during a rendezvous and not handled in the accept statement, it is propagated to both tasks and must be handled in two places. See Section 5.8.

note

There are other ways to prevent PROGRAM_ERROR at a selective wait. These involve leaving at least one alternative unguarded, or proving that at least one guard will evaluate TRUE under all circumstances. The point here is that you, or your successors, will make mistakes in trying to do this, so you should prepare to handle the inevitable exception.

6.2.2   Attributes 'COUNT, 'CALLABLE and 'TERMINATED

guideline

- Do not depend on the values of the task attributes 'CALLABLE or 'TERMINATED [18].

- Do not use task attributes to avoid TASKING_ERROR on an entry call.

- Do not depend on the value of the entry attribute 'COUNT.

example

This task needs at least two calls on one entry not coinciding with any calls on the other entry as a prerequisite for an action. It is badly programmed, since it relies upon the values of the 'COUNT attributes not changing between evaluating and acting upon them.

```
---------------------------------------------------------------------
task body INTERCEPT is
   ...
   select
      when (LAUNCH'COUNT > 1) and
           (RECALL'COUNT  = 0)       =>
         accept LAUNCH;
         accept LAUNCH;
         ...
   or
      accept RECALL;
      ...
   end select;
   ...
---------------------------------------------------------------------
```

If the following code is preempted between evaluating the condition and initiating the call, the assumption that the task is still callable may no longer be valid.

```
if INTERCEPT'CALLABLE then
    INTERCEPT.RECALL;
 ...
```

rationale

Attributes 'CALLABLE and 'TERMINATED behave as "sticky bits." They convey reliable information once 'CALLABLE becomes FALSE and once 'TERMINATED becomes TRUE. Otherwise, 'TERMINATED and 'CALLABLE can change between the time your code tests them and the time it responds to the result.

If you reference a task through an access value, another task can execute an allocator between your interrogation of these attributes and your acting upon their values. Should this occur, the attributes may not appear to behave as sticky bits, thus rendering them utterly useless.

The Ada LRM [28] itself warns about the asynchronous increase and decrease of the value of 'COUNT. A task can be removed from an entry queue due to execution of an abort statement as well as expiration of a timed entry call. The use of this attribute in guards of a selective wait statement may result in the opening of alternatives which should not be opened under a changed value of 'COUNT.

exceptions

Use extreme care.

6.2.3   Shared Variables

guideline

- Do not share variables.

- Have tasks communicate through the rendezvous mechanism.

- Do not use shared variables as a task synchronization device.

- Use pragma SHARED only when forced to by run time system deficiencies.

example

This code will print the same line more than once on some occasions and fail to print some lines on other occasions.

```
--------------------------------------------------------------------
task body LINE_PRINTER_DRIVER is
   ...
begin
   loop
      CURRENT_LINE := LINE_BUFFER;
      -- send to device
   end loop;
end LINE_PRINTER_DRIVER;
--------------------------------------------------------------------
task body SPOOL_SERVER is
   ...
begin
   loop
      DISK_READ(SPOOL_FILE, LINE_BUFFER):
   end loop;
end SPOOL_SERVER;
--------------------------------------------------------------------
```

rationale

There are many techniques for protecting and synchronizing data access. You must program most of them yourself to use them. It is difficult to write a program that shares data correctly; if it is not done correctly, the reliability of the program suffers. Ada provides the rendezvous to support communication of information between and synchronization of tasks. Data that you might be tempted to share can be put into a task body with read and write entries to access it.

Some implementations of the rendezvous will not meet time constraints. For this eventuality, Ada also provides pragma SHARED, which presumably has less overhead than the rendezvous, and will implement correctly some data access synchronization technique that you might get wrong. Pragma SHARED can serve as an expedient against poor run time support systems. Programs containing tasks that read or update shared data are erroneous unless non-interference can be guaranteed. Do not use this as an excuse always to avoid the rendezvous, however, because implementations are allowed to ignore pragma SHARED [18]. In addition, if shared variables are used as a buffer, pragma SHARED does not offer mutual exclusion for simultaneous access. Rather, it affects only objects for which storage and retrieval are implemented as indivisible operations.

note

As we pointed out above, a guarantee of non-interference may be difficult with implementations that ignore pragma SHARED. If you must share data, share the absolute minimum amount of data necessary, and be especially careful. As always, encapsulate the synchronization portions of code.

The problem is with variables. Constants, such as tables fixed at compile time, may be safely shared between tasks.

6.2.4 Tentative Rendezvous Constructs

guideline

- Avoid conditional entry calls.
- Avoid selective waits with else parts.
- Avoid timed entry calls.
- Avoid selective waits with delay alternatives.

rationale

Use of these constructs always poses a risk of race conditions. Their use in loops, particularly with poorly chosen task priorities, can have the effect of busy waiting.

These constructs are very much implementation dependent. For conditional entry calls and selective waits with else parts, the Ada LRM [28] does not define "immediately." For timed entry calls and selective waits with delay alternatives, implementors may have ideas of time that differ from each other and from your own.

6.2.5 Communication Complexity

guideline

- Minimize the number of accept and select statements per task.
- Minimize the number of accept statements per entry.

example

```
-- use
      accept A;
      if MODE_1 then
         -- do one thing
      else -- MODE_2
         -- do something different
      end if;

-- rather than
      if MODE_1 then
         accept A do
            -- do one thing
            ...
      else -- MODE_2
         accept A do
            -- do something different
      end if;
```

rationale

This guideline is motivated by reduction of conceptual complexity. With small numbers of accept or select statements, the programmer of the task and the programmer of the calling units need not reason about the circumstances of an entry call executing different code sequences dependent on the task's local state. In addition to the reduction in conceptual complexity, the size of the resulting source code for the task body can be controlled. Finally, a large number of accept and select statements carries with it a large amount of inter-task communication, with its inevitable overhead. It could be that tasks which need to communicate very frequently are poorly designed. The communication overhead should, in general, be insignificant compared with the independent, parallel computation.

6.3   TERMINATION

The ability of tasks to interact with each other using Ada's inter-task communication features makes it especially important to manage planned or unplanned (e.g., in response to a catastrophic exception condition) termination in a disciplined way. To do otherwise can lead to a proliferation of undesired and unpredictable side effects as a result of the termination of a single task.

6.3.1   Normal Termination

guideline

- Do not create non-terminating tasks [18] unless you really mean it.

- Explicitly shut down tasks dependent on library units.

example

This task will never terminate:

```
------------------------------------------------------------------------
task body MESSAGE_BUFFER is
   ...
begin -- MESSAGE_BUFFER
   loop
      select
         when ( HEAD /= TAIL )
            => accept RETRIEVE ( ...
      or
         when not(((HEAD = LOWER_BOUND          )and then
                   (TAIL = UPPER_BOUND          )         )or else
                  ((HEAD/= LOWER_BOUND          )and then
                   (TAIL = BUFFER'RANGE'PRED(HEAD))        )        )
            => accept STORE ( ...
      end select;
   end loop;
end MESSAGE_BUFFER;
------------------------------------------------------------------------
```

rationale

A non–terminating task is a task whose body consists of a non–terminating loop with no selective wait with terminate, or a task that is dependent on a library unit. Execution of a subprogram or block containing a task cannot complete until the task terminates. Any task that calls a subprogram containing a non–terminating task will be delayed indefinitely.

The effect of unterminated tasks at the end of program execution is undefined. A task dependent on a library unit cannot be forced to terminate using a selective wait with terminate and should be terminated explicitly during program shutdown. One way to terminate tasks dependent on library units is to provide them with exit entries. Have the main subprogram call the exit entry just before it terminates.

exceptions

If you are simulating a cyclic executive, you may need a scheduling task that does not terminate. It has been said that no real–time system should be programmed to terminate. This is extreme. Systematic shut–down of many real–time systems is a desirable safety feature.

If you are considering programming a task not to terminate, be certain that it is not a dependent of a block or subprogram from which its caller(s) will ever expect to return. In light of the fact that entire programs can be candidates for reuse (see Chapter 8), document the fact that the task (and whatever it depends upon) will not terminate. Also be certain that for any other task that you do wish to terminate, its termination does not await this task's termination. Reread and fully understand the language reference manual [28] § 9.4 on "Task Dependence – Termination of Tasks."

6.3.2   The Abort Statement

guideline

- Avoid using the abort statement.

rationale

When an abort statement is executed, there is no way to know what the targeted task was doing beforehand. Data for which the target task is responsible may be left in an inconsistent state. It is possible for a task to mistakenly execute abort statements targeting tasks it does not intend, including itself, due to aliases or the tree of task dependency. Further, the abort statement is not useful for dealing with tasks that are no longer accessible (see Guideline 6.1.3).

The purposes of the abort statement are to stop a "runaway" or malfunctioning task, and to free up processor resources quickly in an emergency or extremely time–critical situation. It can be very difficult to determine whether a task is malfunctioning. There is no guarantee that the task making that determination is not itself malfunctioning. The determination of what constitutes an emergency is both difficult and political. The rare emergency situations should already have been made quite clear in the requirements or specification of the software system. Beware of making these decisions yourself.

An implementation is not required to do much to a task which is the target of an abort statement until the task reaches a synchronization point. Consequently, the purposes of freeing up processor resources and stopping runaway tasks can be subverted. The latter is particularly futile in the case of a task in an infinite loop, as it may never reach a synchronization point.

6.3.3   Programmed Termination

guideline

- Use a select statement rather than an accept statement alone.

- Provide a terminate alternative for <u>every</u> selective wait that does not require an else part or a delay.

rationale

To do otherwise is to court deadlock. Execution of an accept statement or of a selective wait statement without an else part, a delay, or a terminate alternative cannot proceed if no task ever calls the entry(s) associated with that statement. Following this guideline entails programming multiple termination points in the task body. A reader can easily "know where to look" for the normal termination points in a task body. The termination points are the end of the body's sequence of statements, and alternatives of select statements.

6.3.4   Abnormal Termination

guideline

- Place an exception handler for others at the end of a task body.

- Have each exception handler at the end of a task body report the task's demise.

example

This is one of many tasks updating the positions of blips on a radar screen. When started, it is given part of the name by which its parent knows it. Should it terminate due to an exception, it signals the fact in one of its parent's data structures.

```
------------------------------------------------------------------------
task body TRACK is
   MY_INDEX : TRACKS := NEUTRAL;
   ...
begin -- TRACK
   select
      accept START(WHO_AM_I : TRACKS) do
         MY_INDEX := WHO_AM_I;
      end START;
   or
      TERMINATE;
   end select;
   ...
exception
   when others =>
      if MY_INDEX /= NEUTRAL then
         STATION(MY_INDEX).STATUS := DEAD;
      end if;
end TRACK;
------------------------------------------------------------------------
```

rationale

Unless a task reports the fact, it will become completed if an exception is raised within it for which it has no handler. Remember that exceptions are not propagated out of tasks. Providing exception handlers, and especially a handler for others, ensures that a task can always regain control. Having a task report its demise allows other tasks to start recovery from its loss. An unhandled exception in a task body would circumvent the chance to report. Thus the need for an others handler to catch it.

6.4   SUMMARY

tasking

- Use tasks to model abstract, asynchronous entities within the problem domain.
- Use tasks to control or synchronize access to tasks or other asynchronous entities (e.g., asynchronous I/O, peripheral devices, interrupts).
- Use tasks to define concurrent algorithms.
- Use tasks to perform cyclic or prioritized activities.
- Do not use anonymous task types.
- Differentiate between static and dynamic tasks.
- Use caution with dynamically allocated task objects.
- Avoid referencing terminated tasks through their aliases.
- Avoid disassociating a task from all names.

- Do not use the pragma PRIORITY to handle synchronization.

- Do not depend on a particular delay being achievable.

- Never use a busy waiting loop instead of a delay.

- Design to limit polling to those cases where absolutely necessary.

- Never use knowledge of the execution pattern of tasks to achieve timing requirements.

communication

- Provide a handler for exception PROGRAM_ERROR wherever there is no else part in a selective wait statement.

- Make systematic use of handlers for TASKING_ERROR.

- Be prepared to handle exceptions during a rendezvous.

- Do not depend on the values of the task attributes 'CALLABLE or 'TERMINATED.

- Do not use task attributes to avoid TASKING_ERROR on an entry call.

- Do not depend on the value of the entry attribute 'COUNT.

- Do not share variables.

- Have tasks communicate through the rendezvous mechanism.

- Do not use shared variables as a task synchronization device.

- Use pragma SHARED only when forced to by run time system deficiencies.

- Avoid conditional entry calls.

- Avoid selective waits with else parts.

- Avoid timed entry calls.

- Avoid selective waits with delay alternatives.

- Minimize the number of accept and select statements per task.

- Minimize the number of accept statements per entry.

termination

- Do not create non-terminating tasks unless you really mean it.

- Explicitly shut down tasks dependent on library units.

- Avoid using the abort statement.

- Use a select statement rather than an accept statement alone.

- Provide a terminate alternative for every selective wait that does not require an else part or a delay.

- Place an exception handler for others at the end of a task body.

- Have each exception handler at the end of a task body report the task's demise.

Chapter 7

Portability

The manner in which the Ada language has been defined and tightly controlled is intended to provide considerable aid in the portability of Ada programs. In most programming languages, different dialects are prevalent as vendors extend or dilute a language for various reasons such as conformance to a programming environment or to a particular application domain. The Ada Compiler Validation Capability (ACVC) [1], was developed by the U.S. Department of Defense to ensure that implementors strictly adhered to the Ada standard. Although the ACVC mechanism is very beneficial and does eliminate many portability problems that plague other languages, there is a tendency for new Ada users to expect it to eliminate <u>all</u> portability problems; it definitely does not. Certain areas of Ada are not covered by validation. The semantics of Ada leave certain details to the implementor. The implementor's choices with respect to these details affect portability.

There are some general principles to enhancing portability exemplified by many of the guidelines in this chapter. They are:

- <u>Recognize</u> those Ada constructs that may adversely impact portability.

- <u>Avoid</u> the use of these constructs where possible.

- <u>Localize and encapsulate</u> non-portable features of a program if their use is essential.

- <u>Highlight</u> use of constructs that may cause portability problems.

These guidelines cannot be applied thoughtlessly. Many of them involve a detailed understanding of the Ada model and its implementation. In many cases you will have to make carefully considered tradeoffs between efficiency and portability. Reading this chapter should improve your insight into the issues involved.

The material in this chapter was largely acquired from three sources: the ARTEWG Catalogue of Ada Run-time Implementation Dependencies [3]; the Nissen and Wallis book on Portability and Style in Ada [18]; and a paper written for the U.S. Air Force by SofTech on Ada Portability Guidelines [19]. The last of these sources, [19], encompasses the other two and provides an in–depth explanation of the issues, numerous examples, and techniques for minimizing portability problems.   An additional reference, [9], is valuable for understanding the latitude allowed implementors of Ada and the criteria often used to make decisions.

The purpose of this chapter is to provide a summary of portability issues in the guideline format of this book. The chapter does not include all issues identified in the references, rather the most significant. For an in–depth presentation, see [19]. A few additional guidelines are presented here and others are elaborated upon where the authors' experience is applicable.

The goal of this chapter is to aid you in writing portable Ada code. There are fewer exceptions provided for the guidelines because many of the guidelines are rules of thumb that have been used effectively in the past.

A recent article addresses Ada I/O portability issues [14]. None of its suggestions were included herein, but it may be of interest.

7.1   FUNDAMENTALS

This section introduces some generally applicable principles of writing portable Ada programs. It includes guidelines about the assumptions you should make with respect to a number of Ada features and their implementations, and guidelines about the use of other Ada features to ensure maximum portability.

7.1.1   Global Assumptions ‡

guideline

- Make considered assumptions about the support an implementation will provide for the following:
  - Number of bits available for type INTEGER.
  - Number of decimal digits of precision available for floating point types.
  - Number of bits available for fixed–point types.
  - Number of characters per line of source text.
  - Number of bits for *universal_integer* expressions.
  - Number of seconds for the range of DURATION.
  - Number of milliseconds for DURATION'SMALL.

example

These are minimum values (or minimum precision in the case of DURATION′SMALL) that a project or application might assume that an implementation will provide. There is no guarantee that a given implementation will provide more than the minimum, so these would be treated by the project or application as maximum values also.

- 16 bits available for type INTEGER.

- 6 decimal digits of precision available for floating point types.

- 32 bits available for fixed-point types.

- 72 characters per line of source text.

- 16 bits for *universal_integer* expressions.

- -86_400 .. 86_400 seconds (1 day) for the range of DURATION.

- 20 milliseconds for DURATION′SMALL.

rationale

Some assumptions must be made with respect to certain implementation dependent values. If this is not done, portability might be enhanced for a few obscure machines of historic interest but with an enormous cost in programming complexity. The exact values assumed should cover the majority of the target equipment of interest.

note

Of the microcomputers currently available for incorporation within embedded systems, 16-bit processors are still very prevalent. Although 4-bit and 8-bit machines are still available, their limited memory addressing capabilities make them unsuited to support Ada programs of any size. Using current representation schemes, 6 decimal digits of floating point accuracy implies a representation mantissa at least 21 bits wide, leaving 11 bits for exponent and sign within a 32-bit representation. This correlates with the data widths of floating point hardware currently available for the embedded systems market. A 32-bit minimum on fixed-point numbers correlates with the accuracy and storage requirements of floating point numbers.

The 72-column limit on source lines in the example is an unfortunate hold-over from the days of Hollerith punched cards with sequence numbers. Much of the current machinery and software used in manipulating source code is still bound to assumptions about this maximum line length. The 16-bit example for *universal_integer* expressions matches that for INTEGER storage.

The values for the range and accuracy of values of the predefined type DURATION are the limits expressed in the Ada LRM ([28] § 9.6). You should not expect an implementation to provide a wider range or a finer granularity.

7.1.2   Actual Limits

guideline

- Determine the actual properties and limits of the Ada implementation(s) you are using.

rationale

The Ada model may not match exactly with the underlying hardware so some compromises may have been made in the implementation; check to see if they could affect your program. Particular implementations may do "better" than the Ada model requires; while some others may be just minimally acceptable. Arithmetic is generally implemented with a precision higher than the storage capacity (this is implied by the Ada type model for floating point).   Different implementations may behave differently on the same underlying hardware.

7.1.3   Non–Standard Character Sets

guideline

- Avoid idiosyncrasies of non–standard character sets.

rationale

An implementation is only required to recognize characters from the ISO extended character set. Using a different character set could make the source text unreadable.

7.1.4   Documentation

guideline

- Use highlighting comments for each package, subprogram and task where any non–portable features are present.

- For each non–portable feature employed, describe the expectations for that feature.

example

```
-----------------------------------------------------------------------
with SYSTEM;
package MEMORY_MAPPED_IO is
-- WARNING - This package is implementation specific.
-- It uses absolute memory addresses to interface with the I/O system.
-- It assumes a particular printer's line length.
-- Change memory mapping and printer details when porting.

    PRINTER_LINE_LENGTH : constant := 132;
    type DATA is array(1..PRINTER_LINE_LENGTH) of CHARACTER;
    procedure WRITE_LINE (LINE : in DATA);
end MEMORY_MAPPED_IO;
-----------------------------------------------------------------------
package body MEMORY_MAPPED_IO is
-----------------------------------------------------------------------
    procedure WRITE_LINE (LINE : in DATA) is
        BUFFER : DATA;
        for BUFFER use at SYSTEM.PHYSICAL_ADDRESS(16#200#);
    begin
        -- perform output operation through specific memory locations.
    end WRITE_LINE;
-----------------------------------------------------------------------
end MEMORY_MAPPED_IO;
-----------------------------------------------------------------------
```

rationale

The explicit documentation of each breach of portability will raise its visibility and aid in the porting process. A description of the non-portable feature's expectations covers the common case where vendor documentation of the original implementation is not available to the person performing the porting process.

7.1.5   Main Subprogram

guideline

• Avoid using any implementation features associated with the main subprogram (e.g., allowing parameters to be passed).

rationale

The Ada LRM [28] places very few requirements on the main subprogram. Assuming the simplest case will increase portability. That is, assume you may only use a parameterless procedure as a main program. Some operating systems are capable of acquiring and interpreting returned integer values near zero from a function, but many others cannot. Further, many real-time, embedded systems will not be designed to terminate, so a function or a procedure having parameters with modes out or in out will be inappropriate to such applications.

This leaves procedures with in parameters. Although some operating systems can pass parameters in to a program as it starts, others cannot. Also, an implementation may not be able to perform type checking on such parameters even if the surrounding environment is capable of providing them. Finally, real–time, embedded applications may not have an "operator" initiating the program to supply the parameters, in which case it would be more appropriate for the program to have been compiled with a package containing the appropriate constant values or for the program to read the necessary values from, say, switch settings or a downloaded auxiliary file. In any case, the variation in surrounding initiating environments is far too great to depend upon the kind of last–minute (program) parameterization implied by (subprogram) parameters to the main subprogram.

7.1.6 Encapsulating Implementation Dependencies

guideline

- Encapsulate hardware and implementation dependencies in a package or packages.

- Clearly indicate the objectives if machine or solution efficiency is the reason for hardware or implementation dependent code.

example

See Guideline 7.1.4.

rationale

Encapsulating hardware and implementation dependencies in a package or packages allows the remainder of the code to ignore them and thus to be fully portable. It also localizes the dependencies, making it clear exactly which parts of the code may need to be changed when porting the program.

Some implementation dependent features may be used to achieve particular performance or efficiency objectives. Documenting these objectives ensures that the programmer will find an appropriate way to achieve them when porting to a different implementation, or explicitly recognize that they cannot be achieved.

note

Ada can be used to write machine dependent programs that take advantage of an implementation in a manner consistent with the Ada model, but which make particular choices where Ada allows implementation freedom. These machine dependencies should be treated in the same way as any other implementation dependent features of the code.

7.1.7   Location of Program Unit Specification and Body

guideline

- Separate, but be prepared to combine, the specification of a package and its body.

rationale

Separation of package specification and body is desirable for a number of reasons (see Guideline 4.1.1). In the context of portability, an important reason is to facilitate the provision of multiple bodies for the same specification, one body for each target machine.

An implementation is permitted to require that the two be part of the same compilation. The reasons for separation are compelling, particularly in light of the ease with which you can catenate them upon input to compilers on so many host systems.

7.1.8   Custom Bodies

guideline

- Develop specific bodies for specific applications to meet particular needs or constraints after porting.

rationale

When more is known about the details of a particular problem and the target hardware, a specific, custom–built routine can almost always do better in at least some respects than a general purpose routine that was acquired by porting. It is in keeping with the Ada philosophy to develop a program in a general way and later customize it through the use of specialized bodies.

7.1.9   Verifying a Port

guideline

- Do not rely on testing to show correctness of a port.

rationale

In general, no amount of testing can find all the potential errors in a program. Ada allows variations in implementations that may render a particular implementation incapable of demonstrating the error. This can lead to a false sense that the program is correct. However, when the program is ported, the fault may manifest itself because of a change in the underlying implementation. If it is known that correct behavior of a program depends on some aspect of the implementation outside the minimal Ada requirements, the details need to be carefully documented.

7.1.10 Incorrect Order Dependencies

guideline

- Avoid depending on the order in which certain constructs in Ada are evaluated (see [28] index, page I-17 for list).

example

This example intentionally violates some of our guidelines, including naming, use of non-local variables, and side-effects. The important thing, here, is that the commented line depends on "Y" being evaluated before "SQUARE(Y)".

```
X, Y : REAL;
...
------------------------------------------------------------------------
function SQUARE (in VALUE : REA ) return REAL is
begin
   Y := VALUE * VALUE;
   return Y;
end SQUARE;
------------------------------------------------------------------------
...
X := Y + SQUARE( Y ); -- sum Y and its square; make Y contain square of
                      -- its former self; keep the sum in X.
```

rationale

An incorrect order dependency may arise whenever the Ada LRM [28], "...specifies that different parts of a given construct are to be executed *in some order that is not specified by the language*[. T]he construct is incorrect if execution of these parts in a different order would have a different effect" ([28], §1.6).

While an incorrect order dependency may not adversely effect the program on a certain implementation, when it is ported the code might not execute correctly. Avoid incorrect order dependencies, but also recognize that even an unintentional error of this kind could prohibit portability.

7.2 NUMERIC TYPES AND EXPRESSIONS

A great deal of care was taken with the design of the Ada features related to numeric computations to ensure that the language could be used in embedded systems and mathematical applications where precision was important. As far as possible, these features were made portable; however there is an inevitable tradeoff between maximally exploiting the available precision of numeric computation on a particular machine and maximizing the portability of Ada numeric constructs. This means that these Ada features, particularly numeric types and expressions, must be used with great care if full portability of the resulting program is to be guaranteed.

7.2.1 Predefined Numeric Types

guideline

- Do not use the predefined numeric types in package STANDARD. Use range and digits declarations and let the implementation do the derivation <u>implicitly</u> from the predefined types.

- For programs that require greater accuracy than that provided by the global assumptions, define a package that declares a private type and operations as needed (see [19] for a full explanation and examples).

example

```
-- use
type DAY_OF_LEAP_YEAR is range 1 .. 366;
-- rather than
type DAY_OF_LEAP_YEAR is new INTEGER range 1 .. 366;
```

The latter is not representable as a subrange of INTEGER on a machine with an 8–bit word. The former allows a compiler to choose a multiword representation if necessary.

rationale

An implementor is free to define the range of the predefined numeric types. Porting code from an implementation with greater accuracy to one of lesser is a time consuming and error–prone process. Many of the errors are not reported until run–time.

This applies to more than just numerical computation. An easy-to-overlook instance of this problem occurs if you neglect to use explicitly declared types for integer discrete ranges (array sizes, loop ranges, etc.) (see Guidelines 5.5.1 and 5.5.2). If you do not provide an explicit type when specifying index constraints and other discrete ranges, a predefined integer type is assumed.

exceptions

The private type and related operations approach can incur considerable overhead. Apply alternative techniques (e.g., subtypes) to those portions of a program requiring greater efficiency.

7.2.2 Ada Model

guideline

- Know the Ada model for floating point types and arithmetic.

rationale

Declarations of Ada floating point types give users control over both the representation and arithmetic used in floating point operations. Portable properties of Ada programs are derived from the models for floating point numbers of the subtype and the corresponding safe numbers. The relative spacing and range of values in a type are determined by the declaration. Attributes can be used to specify the transportable properties of an Ada floating point type.

7.2.3   Analysis

guideline

- Carefully analyze what accuracy and precision you really need.

rationale

Floating point calculations are done with the equivalent of the implementation's predefined floating point types. The effect of extra "guard" digits in internal computations can sometimes lower the number of digits that must be specified in an Ada declaration. This may not be consistent over implementations where the program is intended to be run. It may also lead to the false conclusion that the declared types are sufficient for the accuracy required.

The numeric type declarations should be chosen to satisfy the lowest precision (smallest number of digits) that will provide the required accuracy. Careful analysis will be necessary to show that the declarations are adequate.

7.2.4   Accuracy Constraints

guideline

- Do not press the accuracy limits of the machine(s).

rationale

The Ada floating point model is intended to facilitate program portability, which is often at the expense of efficiency in the use of the underlying machine arithmetic. Just because two different machines use the same number of digits in the mantissa of a floating point number does not imply they will have the same arithmetic properties. Some Ada implementations may give slightly better accuracy than required by Ada because they make efficient use of the machine. Do not write programs that depend on this.

7.2.5   Commentary

guideline

- Document the analysis and derivation of the numerical aspects of a program.

rationale

Decisions and background about why certain precisions are required in a program are important to program revision or porting. The underlying numerical analysis leading to the program should be documented.

7.2.6 Precision of Constants

guideline

- Use named numbers or universal real expressions rather than constants of any particular type.

rationale

For a given radix (number base), there is a loss of accuracy for some rational and all irrational numbers when represented by a finite sequence of digits. Ada has named numbers and expressions of type *universal_real* that provide maximal accuracy of representation in the source program. These numbers and expressions are converted to finite representations at compile time. By using universal real expressions and numbers, the programmer can automatically delay the conversion to machine types until the point where it can be done with the minimum loss of accuracy.

note

See also Guideline 3.3.5.

7.2.7 Appropriate Radix

guideline

- Represent literals in a radix appropriate to the problem.

example

```
type MAXIMUM_SAMPLES     is range 1         .. 1_000_000;
type LEGAL_HEX_ADDRESS   is range 16#0000#  .. 16#FFFF#;
type LEGAL_OCTAL_ADDRESS is range  8#000_000# .. 8#777_777#;
```

rationale

Ada provides a way of representing numbers using a radix other than ten. These numbers are called based literals ([28] §2.4.2). The choice of radix determines whether the representation of a radix fraction will terminate or repeat. This technique is appropriate when the problem naturally uses some base other than ten for its numbers.

7.2.8   Subexpression Evaluation

guideline

- Anticipate values of subexpressions to avoid exceeding the range of their type. Use derived types, subtypes, factoring, and range constraints on numeric types as described in Guidelines 3.4.1, 5.3.1, 5.5.3 and 5.5.6.

rationale

The Ada language does not require that an implementation perform range checks on subexpressions within an expression. Even if the implementation on your program's current target does not perform these checks, your program may be ported to an implementation that does.

7.2.9   Relational Tests

guideline

- Do relational tests with <= and >= rather than <, >, =, and /=.

rationale

Strict relational comparisons (<, >, =, /=) are a general problem in floating point computations. Because of the way Ada comparisons are defined in terms of model intervals, it is possible for the values of the Ada comparisons A < B and A = B to depend on the implementation, while A <= B evaluates uniformly across implementations. Note that in Ada, "A <= B" is not the same as "not (A > B)".

7.2.10   Type Attributes

guideline

- Use values of type attributes in comparisons and checking for small values.

example

```
if abs(X - Y) <= FLOAT_TYPE'SMALL              -- (1)
if abs(X - Y) <= FLOAT_TYPE'BASE'SMALL         -- (2)
if abs(X - Y) <= abs X * FLOAT_TYPE'EPSILON    -- (3)
if abs(X - Y) <= abs X * FLOAT_TYPE'BASE'EPSILON -- (4)
```

These examples test for (1) absolute "equality" in storage, (2) absolute "equality" in computation, (3) relative "equality" in storage, and (4) relative "equality" in computation.

rationale

These attributes are the primary means of symbolically accessing the implementation of the Ada numeric model. When the characteristics of the model numbers are accessed symbolically, the source code is portable. The appropriate model numbers of any implementation will then be used by the generated code.

7.2.11 Testing Special Operands

guideline

- Test carefully around special values.

rationale

Tests around zero are particularly troublesome; for example, if x is any value mathematically in the range $-T'SMALL < X < T'SMALL$, it is possible for either (and maybe both) of the Ada expressions $x <= 0.0$ or $x >= 0.0$ to evaluate to TRUE.

7.3 STORAGE CONTROL

The management of dynamic storage can vary between Ada implementations. The guidelines in this section encourage the programmer to bring dynamic storage management under explicit program control to improve the portability of programs using it.

7.3.1 Collection Size for Access Types

guideline

- Use a representation clause to specify the collection size for access types. Specify the collection size in general terms using the 'SIZE attribute of the object type.

example

```
type PERSONNEL_INFORMATION is
  record
    -- desired information
  end PERSONNEL_INFORMATION;

type SUBJECT_EMPLOYEE is access PERSONNEL_INFORMATION;

for SUBJECT_EMPLOYEE'STORAGE_SIZE use
  (NUMBER_OF_EMPLOYEES + SLACK)
    * (PERSONNEL_INFORMATION'SIZE / SYSTEM.STORAGE_UNIT);
```

rationale

There are many variations among implementations of dynamic storage algorithms. Here is a brief summary of some of the issues:

- The processing time to acquire the storage and then later free it up (with possible garbage collection) can vary greatly;

- The time at which overhead is incurred (e.g., obtaining a pool at type declaration time versus individual objects when created versus seemingly random garbage collection) varies greatly;

- The total amount of space available to a given scope may be restricted.

- Dynamic storage pools, with Ada runtime implementations that employ them, may be shared among unconstrained arrays, records with discriminants and miscellaneous run–time data structures.

Given this degree of variability it is advantageous to use a representation clause to specify the exact requirements for a given type even though the representation clause is itself an implementation dependent feature.

note

The amount of storage specified using the representation clause need not be static.

exceptions

Some implementations do not give you the exact number of objects requested, but fewer due to allocation scheme overhead. Be certain to provide some headroom for this possibility.

7.3.2   Task Storage

guideline

- Use a representation clause to identify the expected stack space requirements for each task.

rationale

Implementations may vary greatly in the manner in which task stack space is obtained. The varying methods may affect performance or access type storage allocation (when stack space is obtained from heaps).

Even though a representation clause is an optional and implementation–dependent feature (in the worst case it will be ignored), it provides a mechanism for control of dynamic memory allocation with respect to task activation.

7.4   TASKING

The definition of tasking in the Ada language leaves many characteristics of the tasking model up to the implementor. This allows a vendor to make appropriate tradeoffs for the intended application domain, but it also diminishes the portability of designs and code employing the tasking features. In some respects this diminished portability is an inherent characteristic of concurrency approaches (see [18], page 37).

A discussion of Ada tasking dependencies when employed in a distributed target environment is beyond the scope of this book. For example, multi–processor task scheduling, inter–processor rendezvous, and the distributed sense of time through package CALENDAR are all subject to differences between implementations. For more information, [18] and [3] touch on these issues and [29] is one of many research articles available in the literature.

7.4.1   Task Activation Order

guideline

- Do not depend on the order in which task objects are activated when declared in the same declarative list.

rationale

The order is left undefined in the Ada LRM [28].

7.4.2   Delay Statements

guideline

- Do not depend on a particular delay being achievable [18].
- Never use a busy waiting loop instead of a delay.
- Design to limit polling to those cases where it is absolutely necessary.
- Never use knowledge of the execution pattern of tasks to achieve timing requirements.

rationale

The rationale for this appears in Guideline 6.1.5. In addition, however, the treatment of delay statements varies from implementation to implementation thereby hindering portability.

7.4.3   Package CALENDAR, Type DURATION, and SYSTEM.TICK

guideline

- Do not assume a correlation between SYSTEM.TICK and package CALENDAR or type DURATION (see Guideline 6.1.5).

rationale

Such a correlation is not required, although it may exist in some implementations.

7.4.4   Select Statement Evaluation Order

guideline

- Do not depend on the order in which guard conditions are evaluated or on the algorithm for choosing among several open select alternatives.

rationale

The language does not define the order of these conditions, so assume that they are arbitrary.

7.4.5   Task Scheduling Algorithm

guideline

- Do not depend on the order in which tasks are executed or the extent to which they are interleaved. Use pragma PRIORITY to distinguish general levels of importance only (see Guideline 6.1.4).

rationale

The Ada tasking model is based on preemption and requires that tasks be synchronized only through the explicit means provided in the language (i.e., Rendezvous, task dependence, and pragma SHARED). The scheduling algorithm is not defined by the language and may vary from time sliced to pre-emptive priority. Some implementations (e.g., VAX Ada) provide several choices that a user may select for the application.

note

The number of priorities may vary between implementations. In addition, the manner in which tasks of the same priority are handled may vary between implementations even if the implementations use the same general scheduling algorithm.

exceptions

In real-time systems it is often necessary to tightly control the tasking algorithm in order to obtain the required performance. For example, avionics systems are frequently driven by cyclic events with limited asynchronous interruptions. A non-preemptive tasking model is traditionally used to obtain the greatest performance in these applications. Cyclic executives can be programmed in Ada, as can a progression of scheduling schemes from cyclic through multiple-frame-rate to full asynchrony [13] although an external clock is usually required.

7.4.6   Abort

guideline

- Avoid using the abort statement.

rationale

The rationale for this appears in Guideline 6.3.2. In addition, however, the treatment of abort varies from implementation to implementation thereby hindering portability.

7.4.7   Shared Variables and Pragma SHARED

guideline

- Do not share variables.

- Have tasks communicate through the rendezvous mechanism.

- Do not use shared variables as a task synchronization device.

- Use pragma SHARED only when forced to by run time system deficiencies.

rationale

The rationale for this appears in Guideline 6.2.3. In addition, however, the treatment of shared variables varies from implementation to implementation thereby hindering portability.

7.5   EXCEPTIONS

Care must be exercised using predefined exceptions as aspects of their treatment may vary between implementations. Implementation defined exceptions must, of course, be avoided.

7.5.1   Predefined Exceptions

guideline

- Don't depend on the exact locations at which predefined exceptions are raised.

rationale

The Ada LRM [28] gives sufficient freedom to implementors that in many cases a predefined exception for the same cause can be raised from a number of locations. You will not be able to discriminate between them. Further, each of the predefined exceptions is associated with a variety of conditions. Any exception handler written for a predefined exception must be prepared to deal with any of these conditions.

7.5.2   CONSTRAINT_ERROR and NUMERIC_ERROR

guideline

- Program for the possibility of either CONSTRAINT_ERROR or NUMERIC_ERROR.

rationale

Either of these exceptions may be raised (and different implementations may raise either one under otherwise similar circumstances). Exception handlers should be prepared to handle either.

7.5.3   Implementation–defined Exceptions

guideline

- Do not use implementation–defined exceptions.

rationale

No exception defined by an implementation can be guaranteed portable to other implementations whether or not from the same vendor. Not only may the names be different, but the range of conditions triggering the exceptions may be different also.

exceptions

If you create interface packages for the implementation–specific portions of your program, you can have those packages "export" the implementation–defined exceptions, or better, define user exceptions. Keep the names you use for these general. Do not allow yourself to be forced to find and change the name of every handler you have written for these exceptions when the program is ported.

7.6   REPRESENTATION CLAUSES AND IMPLEMENTATION–DEPENDENT FEATURES

Ada provides many implementation dependent features that permit greater control over and interaction with the underlying hardware architecture than is normally provided by a high–order language. These mechanisms are intended to assist in systems programming and real–time programming to obtain greater efficiency (e.g., specific size layout of variables through representation clauses) and direct hardware interaction (e.g., interrupt entries) without having to resort to assembly level programming.

Given the objectives for these features, it is not surprising that you must usually pay a significant price in portability to use them. In general, where portability is the main objective, do not use these features. When you must use these features, encapsulate them in packages well–documented as interfacing to the particular target environment.

This section identifies the various features and their recommended use with respect to portability.

7.6.1   Representation Clauses

guideline

- Avoid the use of representation clauses.

rationale

The Ada LRM [28] does not require that these clauses be supported for all types.

exceptions

The two exceptions to this guideline are for task storage size and access collection size, where portability may be enhanced through their use (see Guidelines 7.3.1 and 7.3.2).

7.6.2   Interrupt Entries

guideline

- Isolate interrupt receiving tasks into implementation dependent packages.
- Pass the interrupt to the main tasks via a normal entry.
- Use named constants for representation clause interrupt values.
- Place representation–clause named constants in an implementation dependent package.

rationale

Interrupt entries are implementation dependent features that may not be supported (e.g., VAX Ada uses pragmas to assign system traps to "normal" rendezvous). However, interrupt entries cannot be avoided in most embedded real–time systems and it is reasonable to assume that they are supported by an Ada implementation. The actual value for an interrupt is implementation defined. Isolate it.

exceptions

The isolation of interrupt entries creates an additional rendezvous that will often double the interrupt latency time. Where this is unacceptable, the interrupt entries must be proliferated with a resulting decrease in portability. The isolation of the interrupt value named constants will not affect performance and provides portability between similarly supported implementations.

7.6.3   Package SYSTEM

guideline

- Avoid the use of package SYSTEM constants except in attempting to generalize other machine dependent constructs.

rationale

Since the values in this package are implementation provided, unexpected effects can result from their use.

exceptions

Do use package SYSTEM constants to parameterize other implementation dependent features (see [19] examples for numeric ranges (§13.7.1) and access collection size (§4.8)).

7.6.4   Machine Code Inserts

guideline

- Avoid machine code inserts.

rationale

There is no requirement that this feature be implemented. It is possible that two different vendors' syntax would differ for an identical target and certainly, differences in lower-level details such as register conventions would hinder portability.

exceptions

If machine code inserts must be used to meet another project requirement, recognize the portability decreasing effects and isolate and highlight their use.

Include in the commentary that a machine code insert is being used, what function the insert provides, and (especially) why the insert is necessary. Document the necessity of using machine code inserts by delineating what went wrong with attempts to use other, higher-level constructs.

7.6.5   Interfacing Foreign Languages

guideline

- Avoid interfacing Ada with other languages.
- Isolate all subprograms employing pragma INTERFACE to an implementation-dependent (interface) package.

rationale

The problems with employing pragma INTERFACE are complex. These problems include pragma syntax differences, conventions for linking/binding Ada to other languages, and mapping Ada variables to foreign language variables, among others.

exceptions

It is often necessary to interact with other languages, if only an assembly language to reach certain hardware features. In these cases, clearly document the requirements and limitations of the interface and pragma INTERFACE usage.

7.6.6   Implementation–defined Pragmas And Attributes

guideline

- Avoid pragmas and attributes added by the implementor.

rationale

The Ada LRM [28] permits an implementor to add pragmas and attributes to exploit a particular hardware architecture or software environment. These are obviously even more implementation specific and therefore less portable than are an implementor's interpretations of the predefined pragmas and attributes.

exceptions

Some implementation dependent features are gaining wide acceptance in the Ada community to help alleviate inherent inefficiencies in some Ada features. A good example of this is the "fast interrupt" mechanism that provides a minimal interrupt latency time in exchange for a restrictive tasking environment. Ada community groups (e.g. SIGAda's ARTEWG) are attempting to standardize a common mechanism and syntax to provide this capability. By being aware of industry trends, when specialized features must be used, you can take a more general approach that will help minimize the porting task.

7.6.7   Unchecked Deallocation

guideline

- Avoid the use of UNCHECKED_DEALLOCATION (see Guideline 5.9.2).

rationale

The unchecked storage deallocation mechanism is one method for over-riding the default time at which allocated storage is reclaimed. The earliest default time is when an object is no longer accessible, e.g., when control leaves the scope where an access type was declared (the exact point after this time is implementation dependent). Any unchecked deallocation of storage performed prior to this may result in an erroneous Ada program if an attempt is made to access the object.

This guideline is stronger than Guideline 5.9.2 because of the extreme dependence on the implementation of UNCHECKED_DEALLOCATION. Its use could cause considerable difficulty with portability.

exceptions

The use of unchecked deallocation of storage can be beneficial in local control of highly iterative or recursive algorithms where available storage may be exceeded. Take care to avoid erroneous situations as described above.

7.6.8   Unchecked Conversion

guideline

- Avoid the use of UNCHECKED_CONVERSION (see Guideline 5.9.1).

rationale

The unchecked type conversion mechanism is, in effect, a means of by-passing the strong typing facilities in Ada. An implementation is free to limit the types that may be matched and the results that occur when object sizes differ.

exceptions

Unchecked type conversion is useful in implementation dependent parts of Ada programs (where lack of portability is isolated) where low-level programming and foreign language interfacing is the objective.

7.6.9   Runtime Dependencies

guideline

- Avoid the direct invocation of or implicit dependence upon an underlying host operating system or Ada run-time support system.

rationale

Features of an implementation not specified in the Ada LRM [28] will usually differ between implementations. Specific implementation-dependent features are not likely to be provided in other implementations. Even if a majority of vendors eventually provide similar features, they are unlikely to have identical formulations. Indeed, different vendors may use the same formulation for (semantically) entirely different features.

It is a good habit to avoid these in all coding. Consider the consequences of including system calls in a program on a host development system. If these calls are not flagged for removal and replacement, the program could go through development and testing only to be unusable when moved to a target environment which lacks the facilities provided by those system calls on the host.

exceptions

In real–time embedded systems, you will often not be able to avoid making calls to low–level support system facilities. Isolate the uses of these facilities. Document them as you would machine code inserts (see Guideline 7.6.4); they are in a sense instructions for the virtual machine provided by the support system. When isolating the uses of these features, provide an interface for the rest of your program to use which can be ported through replacement of the interface's implementation.

7.6.10   System Partitioning

guideline

- Minimize artificial partitioning of an Ada program to exploit specific architectures.

examples

Example architectures with small address spaces include many of the 16–bit architectures such as the U.S. Air Force 1750A or Intel 8086/80186 (where only 128K bytes of the 1–2M bytes is directly addressable) or the U.S. Navy AN/UYK–44 or AN/AYK–14 (where only 64K bytes of the 2–4M bytes is directly addressable).

rationale

For applications whose size exceeds that of the direct address space of the target architecture, it is often necessary for an Ada implementation to force a partitioning that is unnatural to the Ada style (e.g. limited use of context clauses and generic invocation). Most 32–bit architectures are better suited to Ada for this reason and should be selected when available.

exceptions

If a limited address space target must be used, performance considerations may force artificial partitioning.

7.7   INPUT/OUTPUT

The I/O facilities in Ada are not a part of the syntactic definition of the language. The constructs in the language have been used to define a set of packages for this purpose. These packages are not expected to meet all the I/O needs of all applications, in particular embedded systems, but rather serve as a core subset that may be used on straight–forward data, and that can be used as examples of building I/O facilities upon the low–level constructs provided by the language. Providing an I/O definition that could meet the requirements of all applications and integrate with the many existing operating systems would result in unacceptable implementation dependencies.

The types of portability problems encountered with I/O tend to be different for applications running with a host operating system versus embedded targets where the Ada run–time is self–sufficient. Interacting with a host operating system offers the added complexity of co–existing with the host file system structures (e.g., hierarchical directories), access methods (e.g., ISAM) and naming conventions (e.g., logical names and aliases based on the current directory); the section on I/O in [3] provides some twenty examples of this type of dependency. Embedded applications have different dependencies that often tie them to the low level details of their hardware devices.

The major defense against these inherent implementation dependencies in I/O is to try to isolate their functionality in any given application. The majority of the following guidelines are focused in this direction.

7.7.1 Implementation–added Features

guideline

- Avoid the use of additional I/O features provided by a particular vendor.

rationale

Vendor added features are not likely to be provided by other implementations. Even if a majority of vendors eventually provide similar additional features, they are unlikely to have identical formulations. Indeed, different vendors may use the same formulation for (semantically) entirely different features.

exceptions

There are many types of applications that require the use of these features. Examples include: multilingual systems that standardize on a vendor's file system, applications that are closely integrated with vendor products such as user interfaces, and embedded systems for performance reasons. Isolate the use of these features into packages.

7.7.2 NAME and FORM Parameters

guideline

- Use constants and variables as symbolic actuals for the NAME and FORM parameters on the predefined I/O packages. Declare and initialize them in an implementation dependency package.

rationale

The format and allowable values of these parameters on the predefined I/O packages can vary greatly between implementations; isolation of these values facilitates portability. Note that not specifying a FORM string or using a null value does not guarantee portability since the implementation is free to specify defaults.

note

It may be desirable to further abstract the I/O facilities by defining additional CREATE and OPEN procedures that hide the visibility of the FORM parameter entirely (see [19] pp. 54–55).

7.7.3   File Closing

guideline

- Close all files explicitly.

rationale

The Ada LRM ([28] §14.1) states, "The language does not define what happens to external files after completion of the main program (in particular, if corresponding files have not been closed)." The possibilities range from being closed in an anticipated manner to deletion.

The disposition of a closed temporary file may vary, perhaps affecting performance and space availability [3].

7.7.4   I/O on Access Types

guideline

- Avoid performing I/O on access types.

rationale

The Ada LRM [28] does not require that it be supported. When such a value is written, it is placed out of reach of the implementation. Thus it is out of reach of the reliability–enhancing controls of strong type checking.

Consider the meaning of this operation. One possible implementation of the values of access types is virtual addresses. If you write such a value, how can you expect another program to read that value and make any sensible use of it? The value cannot be construed to refer to any meaningful location within the reader's address space, nor can a reader infer any information about the writer's address space from the value read. The latter is the same problem that the writer would have trying to interpret or use the value if it is read back in. To wit, a garbage collection and/or heap compaction scheme may have moved the item formerly accessed by that value, leaving that value "pointing" at space which is now being put to indeterminable uses by the underlying implementation.

7.7.5   Package LOW_LEVEL_IO

guideline

- Minimize and isolate the use of the predefined package LOW_LEVEL_IO.

rationale

LOW_LEVEL_IO is intended to support direct interaction with physical devices that are usually unique to a given host or target environment. In addition, the data types provided to the procedures are implementation defined. This allows vendors to define different interfaces to an identical device.

exceptions

Those portions of an application that must deal with this level of I/O, e.g., device drivers and real-time components dealing with discretes, are inherently non-portable. Where performance allows, structure these components to isolate the hardware interface. Only within these isolated portions is it advantageous to employ the LOW_LEVEL_IO interface which is portable in concept and general procedural interface, if not completely so in syntax and semantics.

7.8   SUMMARY

fundamentals

- Make considered assumptions about the support an implementation will provide for the following:
  - Number of bits available for type INTEGER.
  - Number of decimal digits of precision available for floating point types.
  - Number of bits available for fixed-point types.
  - Number of characters per line of source text.
  - Number of bits for *universal_integer* expressions.
  - Number of seconds for the range of DURATION.
  - Number of milliseconds for DURATION'SMALL.
- Determine the actual properties and limits of the Ada implementation(s) you are using.
- Avoid idiosyncrasies of non-standard character sets.
- Use highlighting comments for each package, subprogram and task where any non-portable features are present.
- For each non-portable feature employed, describe the expectations for that feature.

- Avoid using any implementation features associated with the main subprogram (e.g., allowing parameters to be passed).

- Encapsulate hardware and implementation dependencies in a package or packages.

- Clearly indicate the objectives if machine or solution efficiency is the reason for hardware or implementation dependent code.

- Separate, but be prepared to combine, the specification of a package and its body.

- Develop specific bodies for specific applications to meet particular needs or constraints after porting.

- Do not rely on testing to show correctness of a port.

- Avoid depending on the order in which certain constructs in Ada are evaluated.

numeric types and expressions

- Do not use the predefined numeric types in package STANDARD. Use range and digits declarations and let the implementation do the derivation implicitly from the predefined types.

- For programs that require greater accuracy than that provided by the global assumptions, define a package that declares a private type and operations as needed.

- Know the Ada model for floating point types and arithmetic.

- Carefully analyze what accuracy and precision you really need.

- Do not press the accuracy limits of the machine(s).

- Document the analysis and derivation of the numerical aspects of a program.

- Use named numbers or universal real expressions rather than constants of any particular type.

- Represent literals in a radix appropriate to the problem.

- Anticipate values of subexpressions to avoid exceeding the range of their type.

- Do relational tests with <= and >= rather than <, >, =, and /=.

- Use values of type attributes in comparisons and checking for small values.

- Test carefully around special values.

storage control

- Use a representation clause to specify the collection size for access types. Specify the collection size in general terms using the SIZE attribute of the object type.

- Use a representation clause to identify the expected stack space requirements for each task.

tasking

- Do not depend on the order in which task objects are activated when declared in the same declarative list.

- Do not depend on a particular delay being achievable.

- Never use a busy waiting loop instead of a delay.

- Design to limit polling to those cases where it is absolutely necessary.

- Never use knowledge of the execution pattern of tasks to achieve timing requirements.

- Do not assume a correlation between SYSTEM.TICK and package CALENDAR or type DURATION.

- Do not depend on the order in which guard conditions are evaluated or on the algorithm for choosing among several open select alternatives.

- Do not depend on the order in which tasks are executed or the extent to which they are interleaved. Use pragma PRIORITY to distinguish general levels of importance only.

- Avoid using the abort statement.

- Do not share variables.

- Have tasks communicate through the rendezvous mechanism.

- Do not use shared variables as a task synchronization device.

- Use pragma SHARED only when forced to by run time system deficiencies.

exceptions

- Don't depend on the exact locations at which predefined exceptions are raised.

- Program for the possibility of either CONSTRAINT_ERROR or NUMERIC_ERROR.

- Do not use implementation-defined exceptions.

representation clauses and implementation-dependent features

- Avoid the use of representation clauses.

- Isolate interrupt receiving tasks into implementation dependent packages.

- Pass the interrupt to the main tasks via a normal entry.

- Use named constants for representation clause interrupt values.

- Place representation–clause named constants in an implementation dependent package.

- Avoid the use of package SYSTEM constants except in attempting to generalize other machine dependent constructs.

- Avoid machine code inserts.

- Avoid interfacing Ada with other languages.

- Isolate all subprograms employing pragma INTERFACE to an implementation–dependent (interface) package.

- Avoid pragmas and attributes added by the implementor.

- Avoid the use of UNCHECKED_DEALLOCATION.

- Avoid the use of UNCHECKED_CONVERSION.

- Avoid the direct invocation of or implicit dependence upon an underlying host operating system or Ada run–time support system.

- Minimize artificial partitioning of an Ada program to exploit specific architectures.

input/output

- Avoid the use of additional I/O features provided by a particular vendor.

- Use constants and variables as symbolic actuals for the NAME and FORM parameters on the predefined I/O packages. Declare and initialize them in an implementation dependency package.

- Close all files explicitly.

- Avoid performing I/O on access types.

- Minimize and isolate the use of the predefined package LOW_LEVEL_IO.

Chapter 8

Reusability

One of the design goals of Ada was to facilitate the creation and exploitation of reusable parts in recognition of the potential productivity improvements that reuse can bring. To this end, Ada provides features, such as packages and generics, that facilitate the task of developing reusable code parts, and of adapting and exploiting them when they are available.

The guidelines in this chapter are concerned with how to write and exploit reusable code. The underlying assumption is that reusable parts are rarely built in isolation and are hard to recover from code that was developed without reuse in mind. The guidelines therefore focus on how to produce reusable parts as a by–product of developing software for specific applications.

A reusable part must fulfill a number of different criteria:

- Reusable parts must be of the highest possible quality. They must be correct, reliable and robust. An error or weakness in a reusable part may have far–reaching consequences and it is important that other programmers can have a high degree of confidence in any parts offered for reuse.

- Reusable parts must be understandable. A reusable part should be a model of clarity. The requirements for documenting reusable parts are even more stringent than those for parts specific to a particular application.

- Reusable parts should be adaptable. Frequently, an otherwise reusable part will not exactly fit the needs of the current application and will need some changes to be exploited. Anticipated changes, that is changes that can be reasonably foreseen by the developer of the part, should be provided for as far as possible. Unanticipated change can only be accommodated by carefully structuring a part so that it is as adaptable as possible. Many of the considerations pertaining to maintainability apply. If the code is of high quality, clear and conforms to well established design principles such as information hiding, it will be easier to adapt in unforeseen ways. One way to achieve adaptability is through generality. Providing the complete functionality that a part might need in any context allows a subset of the functionality to be used in a particular context, potentially without error prone changes to the part.

- Reusable parts must be portable. They may be used in unforeseen environments both in the context of completely different programs for different application domains and in the context of different Ada implementations.

Many of the guidelines in this chapter are general in nature, or cross reference and emphasize other guidelines in this book. This is inevitable; the same considerations that affect the quality, clarity, maintainability and portability of code also affect its reusability.

8.1 GENERAL CONSIDERATIONS

This section addresses some general considerations related to reuse. It is intended to encourage "thinking reuse" and maximize the amount and quality of reusable code written and exploited.

8.1.1 Ada Features

guideline

- Exploit the features of the Ada language to write general purpose, adaptable code that has the maximum potential for future reuse.

example

This simple example is part of a screen handling package for ASCII terminals. If designed without reuse in mind, the software might include terminal-specific information. All this information is separated in the example and collected into a package containing specific terminal properties. A second package supplies cursor and screen functions and is easily reused since the terminal-specific information is hidden.

```
------------------------------------------------------------------------
package TERMINAL_PROPERTIES is
    --includes all relevant parameters for specific ASCII terminal
    type ROW_RANGE             is  range 1..24;
    type COLUMN_RANGE          is  range 1..80;
    CURSOR_ROW_OFFSET_CODE     :  constant  := 16#20#;
    CURSOR_COLUMN_OFFSET_CODE  :  constant  := 16#32#;
    --            any other necessary data
end TERMINAL_PROPERTIES;
------------------------------------------------------------------------
```

```
------------------------------------------------------------------------
with TERMINAL_PROPERTIES;
package ASCII_TERMINAL_SCREEN_HANDLING is
    procedure POSITION_CURSOR(ROW    : in TERMINAL_PROPERTIES.ROW_RANGE;
                              COLUMN : in TERMINAL_PROPERTIES.COLUMN_RANGE);
    --uses terminal-specific offset codes for cursor motion
    procedure CLEAR_SCREEN;
    --          any other required operations
end ASCII_TERMINAL_SCREEN_HANDLING;
------------------------------------------------------------------------
```

Consider a disk manager, part of which is shown below, that might be reused. There are several different collections of information that should be hidden to facilitate change and reuse, specifically the disk head scheduling algorithm, the buffer manager, and the details of the actual disk commands for read, write, seek, etc. With proper information hiding, these details are hidden thereby freeing the maximum amount of software for reuse without change and identifying what might have to be adapted for other reuse.

```
------------------------------------------------------------------------
package DISK_OPERATIONS is
    procedure READ(...);            -- read and write operations
    procedure WRITE(...);           -- available to remainder of system
--      any other operations
end DISK_OPERATIONS;
------------------------------------------------------------------------

package body DISK_OPERATIONS is
    ------------------------------------------------------------------------
    procedure SELECT_NEXT_OPERATION is -- disk head scheduling algorithm
    begin
        ...
    end SELECT_NEXT_OPERATION;
    ------------------------------------------------------------------------

    package BUFFER_MANAGER is
        ...
    end BUFFER_MANAGER;
    ------------------------------------------------------------------------

    package ACTUAL_DISK_OPERATION is
        ...
    end ACTUAL_DISK_OPERATION;
    ------------------------------------------------------------------------
end DISK_OPERATIONS;
------------------------------------------------------------------------
```

rationale

Many features of Ada make it particularly suitable for the creation of reusable parts. Packages, visibility control, and separate compilation support modularity and information hiding. (see Guidelines in Sections 4.1, 4.2, 5.3 and 5.7). This allows the separation of application specific parts of the code, maximizing the general purpose parts suitable for reuse, and allows the isolation of design decisions within modules, facilitating change. The Ada type system supports localization of data definitions so that consistent changes are easy to make. Generic units directly support the development of general purpose adaptable code, that can be instantiated to perform specific functions. Using these features carefully, and in conformance to the guidelines in this book, will produce code that is more likely to be reusable.

Be open minded about what might be reusable. Everything from small subprograms or packages to complete systems might prove useful as part of some future application.

8.1.2   Exploiting Existing Software

guideline

- Consider reusing existing software in preference to writing new code.
- Prefer reusing large parts to small.

rationale

Reuse is potentially a cost effective approach to programming. You are already practicing reuse by exploiting the primitives of high level languages. Reuse of existing proven large-scale parts will improve the quality of your code as well as your productivity. It enables you to capitalize on the long term experience of yourself and others.

Larger parts or subsystems often provide substantial functionality, and have well-defined and controlled external interfaces. It may take less effort to reuse an entire subsystem than a single module, and the return in functionality and reliability is greater.

8.1.3   Upgrading and Adaptation

guideline

- Consider upgrading or adapting unsuitable, e.g., non-portable, code if no appropriate reusable part is available.
- If you adapt or upgrade an existing part to reuse it, ensure that the adapted part is suitable for future reuse.

rationale

Well written code, even if not originally intended for reuse, can often be reused after appropriate adaptation. For example, the machine dependencies in some piece of code might already be carefully isolated so that they can be easily changed. Adopting the strategy of upgrading code into a reusable part before exploiting it in your current program will increase the stock of reusable parts available to you and others.

8.1.4   Robustness

guideline

- Code reusable parts to be robust in any context.

example

Suppose you are writing a binary–to–BCD converter, part of which is shown below, and you intend the software be available for reuse. Do not assume that the input will always be in a range that will fit into a specific number of decimal digits. If the number of digits has to be restricted, this is an assumption and compliance should be checked even if you "know" it is not violated by your own use.

```
function BINARY_TO_BCD (BINARY_VALUE : in NATURAL) return BCD_IMAGE is
    MAX_REPRESENTABLE : constant NATURAL := 1999;
begin
    if BINARY_VALUE > MAX_REPRESENTABLE then
        raise OUT_OF_RANGE;
    end if;
    ...
end BINARY_TO_BCD;
```

rationale

Any part that is intended to be used again in another program, especially if the other program is likely to be written by other people, should be robust. It should defend itself against misuse. Defensive checks on input parameters should raise exported exceptions, or in specialized cases, filter the "chaff" out of the input values.

note

You can restrict the ranges of values of the inputs by judicious selection or construction of the types of the formal parameters. When you do so, the compiler–generated checking code may be more efficient than any checks you might write. Indeed, such checking is part of the intent of the strong typing in the language. This presents a challenge, however, for generics where the user of your code will select the types of the parameters. Your code must be constructed so as to deal with any value of any type the user may choose to select for an instantiation.

8.2   UNDERSTANDING AND CLARITY

It is particularly important that parts intended for reuse should be easy to understand. What the part does, how to use it, what anticipated changes might be made to it, and how it works must be immediately apparent from inspection of the documentation and the code itself.

8.2.1   Documenting Reusable Parts

guideline

- Document what a reusable part does.

- Document how to use it.

- Document assumptions made by the part.

- Document features of the part that are likely to change.

example

```
------------------------------------------------------------------------
generic
    type ELEMENT is private;
package BUFFER_MANAGER is
-- FUNCTION:
--  Manages a pool of ELEMENT buffers.
--  Allocate using GET; exception NO_MORE_BUFFERS when violate MORE_BUFFERS
--     exist check.
--  Deallocate using FREE.
--  Destroy buffer contents using PURGE.
--  INSERT ELEMENT into buffer; exception NON_EXISTENT_BUFFER when HANDLE
--     not allocated with GET, COPY or MOVE; exception ALREADY_FULL when no
--     room in buffer.
--  ...
-- USAGE:
--  Declare HANDLEs to attach and manipulate buffers of ELEMENTs.
--  ...
--  Reset pool and destroy all buffers using FINALIZE before program end.
-- ASSUMPTIONS:
--  HANDLE objects initially DEAD. Limited number of buffers.
--  ...
--  FINALIZE called before program end.
-- LIKELY CHANGES:
--  Size of buffer pool.
--  Length of each buffer.
--  ...
```

```
    type HANDLE              is limited private;
    DEAD                     :  constant HANDLE;

    function  MORE_BUFFERS   (BUFFER : in      HANDLE) return BOOLEAN;
    procedure GET            (BUFFER : in out HANDLE);
    NO_MORE_BUFFERS          : exception;

    procedure PURGE          (BUFFER : in out HANDLE);

    procedure FREE           (BUFFER : in out HANDLE);

    function  IS_FULL        (BUFFER : in      HANDLE) return BOOLEAN;
    procedure INSERT         (ITEM   : in out ELEMENT;
                             INTO    : in out HANDLE);

    NON_EXISTENT_BUFFER      : exception;
    ALREADY_FULL             : exception;

    function  IS_EMPTY       (BUFFER : in      HANDLE) return BOOLEAN;
    procedure RETRIEVE       (ITEM   : in out ELEMENT;
                             FROM    : in out HANDLE);

    ALREADY_EMPTY            : exception;

    procedure COPY           (FROM   : in out HANDLE;
                             TO      : in out HANDLE);
    UNREACHABLE_BUFFER       : exception;

    procedure MOVE           (FROM   : in out HANDLE;
                             TO      : in out HANDLE);

    procedure FINALIZE;
-----------------------------------------------------------------------
private
    ...
end BUFFER_MANAGER;
-----------------------------------------------------------------------
```

rationale

A reusable part cannot depend on any application or textual context for understanding; documentation in addition to that recommended by the guidelines in Section 3.2 may be needed.

The documentation should provide application and context independent information describing the behavior of the part so that it can be correctly selected for reuse. It should also provide details of how to use it, state any assumptions that the part makes about the environments in which it will be reused, and identify those features that might be changed to adapt the part for reuse in a specific application.

note

Documentation of the use of the part should include comments delineating the acceptable ranges and relationships of inputs, and of acceptable calling sequences for abstractions having multiple operations (subprograms or task entries).

The goal of such comments is to provide details about how the part is intended to be used. The presence of these comments does not provide an excuse to omit defensive checks. Comments without explicit checks may occur in contexts with compiler-generated type checking enabled and appropriately restrictive formal parameter types. The absence of explicit or compiler-generated checks requires comments explaining, and validating, the assumptions about the use of the part.

If your organization or project has a formal reuse policy, or systematically maintained reuse libraries, you must observe project standards when documenting reusable software.

8.2.2   Application-Independent Naming

guideline

- Select the least restrictive names possible for reusable parts and their identifiers.

example

General purpose stack abstraction:

```
-------------------------------------------------------------------------
package GENERAL_STACK is
    procedure PUSH(...);
    procedure POP(...);
    -- other stack operations and exceptions
end GENERAL_STACK;
-------------------------------------------------------------------------
```

Renamed appropriately for use in current application:

```
-------------------------------------------------------------------------
with GENERAL_STACK;
package CAFETERIA is
    package STACK_OF_TRAYS renames GENERAL_STACK;
    -- etc.
end CAFETERIA;
-------------------------------------------------------------------------
```

rationale

Choosing a general or application-independent name for a reusable part encourages its wide reuse. Renaming the part in the context of a specific application (as in the example) ensures that its use will be clear in that context.

8.2.3   Abbreviations

guideline

- Do not use <u>any</u> abbreviations in identifier or unit names.

rationale

This is a stronger guideline than Guideline 3.1.4. However well documented, an abbreviation may cause confusion in some future reuse context. Even universally accepted abbreviations, such as GMT for Greenwich Mean Time can cause problems and should be used only with great caution.

note

When reusing a part in a specific application consider renaming using abbreviations standard to that application.

8.3   ADAPTABILITY

Reusable parts often need to be changed before they can be used in a specific application. They should therefore be structured so that change is easy and as localized as possible. One way of achieving adaptability is to create general parts with complete functionality, only a subset of which might be needed in a given application. Another is to exploit Ada's generic construct to produce parts which can be appropriately instantiated with different parameters. Both of these approaches avoid the error prone process of adapting a part by changing its code, but have limitations and can carry some overhead.

8.3.1   Functionality

guideline

- Provide complete functionality in a reusable part or set of parts. Build in complete functionality, including end conditions, even if some functionality is not needed in this application.

example

```
INITIALIZE_QUEUE(...          -- initialization operation
if  STACK_FULL(...            -- probing operation
SYMBOL_TABLE.CLOSE_FRAME(...  -- finalization operation
```

rationale

This is particularly important in designing/programming an abstraction. Completeness ensures that you have configured the abstraction correctly, without built-in assumptions about its execution environment. It also assures the proper separation of functions so they will be useful to the current application and, in other combinations, to other applications. It is particularly important that they be available to other applications; remember that they can be "optimized" out of the final version of the current product.

note

The example illustrates end condition functions. An abstraction should be automatically initialized before its user gets a chance to damage it. When that is not possible, it should be supplied with initiation operations. In any case, it needs finalization operations, both explicit and default/automatic. Where possible, probing operations should be provided to determine when limits are about to be exceeded. Probing operations are always preferable to trying to use exceptions to deal with such limits.

It is also useful to provide reset operations for many objects. To see that a reset and an initiation can be different, consider the analogous situation of a "warm boot" and a "cold boot" on a personal computer.

Even if all of these operations are not appropriate for the abstraction, the exercise of considering them will aid in formulating a complete set of operations, others of which may be used by another application.

Some implementations of the language link all routines into the executable image, ignoring whether they are used or not, making unused operations a liability. (See Guideline 8.3.10). In such cases, where the overhead is significant, create a copy of the fully functional part and comment out the unused operations with an indication that they are redundant in this application.

8.3.2   Generic Units

guideline

- Make every unit that you write a generic unit if its reuse is even a remote possibility.

- Anticipate change, and use generic parameters to facilitate adaptation of generic units

example

This example is taken from Section 12.4 of the Ada LRM [28].

```
--------------------------------------------------------------------
generic
   SIZE : POSITIVE;
   type ITEM is private;
package STACK is
   procedure PUSH (E : in   ITEM);
   procedure POP  (E : out  ITEM);
   OVERFLOW, UNDERFLOW : exception;
end STACK;
--------------------------------------------------------------------
```

```
package body STACK is

    type TABLE is array (POSITIVE range <>) of ITEM;
    SPACE : TABLE(1 .. SIZE);
    INDEX : NATURAL := 0;
-----------------------------------------------------------------
    procedure PUSH(E : in ITEM) is
    begin
       if INDEX >= SIZE then
          raise OVERFLOW;
       end if;
       INDEX := INDEX + 1;
       SPACE(INDEX) := E;
    end PUSH;
-----------------------------------------------------------------
    procedure POP(E : out ITEM) is
    begin
       if INDEX = 0 then
          raise UNDERFLOW;
       end if;
       E := SPACE(INDEX);
       INDEX := INDEX - 1;
    end POP;
-----------------------------------------------------------------
end STACK;
-----------------------------------------------------------------
```

Instances of this generic package can be obtained as follows:

```
package STACK_INT   is new STACK(SIZE => 200, ITEM => INTEGER);
package STACK_BOOL  is new STACK(100, BOOLEAN);
```

Thereafter, the procedures of the instantiated packages can be called as follows:

```
STACK_INT.PUSH(N);
STACK_BOOL.PUSH(TRUE);
```

Note how simply two entirely different stack packages were obtained from this generic package. Although a similar effect could have been obtained, in principle, by copying the text of a non-generic package and modifying the various types, this is time consuming and very error prone. Little additional effort was required to make the package generic and reuse was enhanced greatly. Reuse of the package by others who need stack data structures is also very simple.

rationale

Making a subprogram or package generic greatly facilitates its reuse. The generic facilities in Ada provide some support within the language for reuse. The generic parameter mechanism allows for adaption of generic units. Attempting to achieve the same effect using an editor or similar tool is less convenient and defeats the checking that the compiler can perform.

note

It may seem that the effort involved in writing generic rather than non-generic units is substantial. However, making units generic is not much more difficult or time consuming than making them non-generic once one becomes familiar with the generic facilities. It is, for the most part, a matter of practice. Also, any effort put into the development of the unit will be recouped when the unit is reused, as it surely will be if it is placed in a reuse library with sufficient visibility. Don't limit your thinking about potential reuse to the application you are working on or to other applications with which you are very familiar. Applications with which you are not familiar or future applications might be able to reuse your software.

8.3.3   Generic Type Parameters

guideline

- Exploit Ada's generic construct to create readily adaptable parts that can be instantiated to operate on different types of data.

example

See example for Guideline 8.3.2.

rationale

It is often possible to increase the potential for reuse by removing the dependence of the software on certain types. Essentially what is being done is to take account of those parts of the software that might need to be adapted for reuse and using the language mechanism to support the adaptation.

8.3.4   Generic Subprogram Parameters

guideline

- Exploit Ada's generic construct to create readily adaptable parts that can be instantiated to provide specific functionality using generic subprogram parameters.

example

This is the specification of a generic sort package. The relational operator that defines ordering is a parameter to the package to allow order to be defined in a use-specific way.

```
-------------------------------------------------------------------
generic
    type ELEMENT is private;
    type DATA     is array (POSITIVE range <>) of ELEMENT;
    with function "<" (LEFT, RIGHT : ELEMENT) return BOOLEAN is <>;
package SORT_FACILITIES is

    procedure QUICK_SORT (DATA_TO_SORT:  in out DATA);

    -- other facilities

end SORT_FACILITIES;
-------------------------------------------------------------------
```

rationale

It is often possible to increase the potential for reuse by removing the dependence of the software on certain key operations. Essentially what is being done is to take account of those parts of the software that might need to be adapted for reuse and using the language mechanism to support the adaptation.

8.3.5   Iterators

guideline

• Provide iterators for traversing complex data structures within reusable parts.

example

```
-------------------------------------------------------------------
generic
    type ELEMENTS is private;
package LIST_MANAGER is

    type LISTS is limited private;
    procedure INSERT (LIST    : in out LISTS;
                      ELEMENT : in     ELEMENTS);

    -- this defines a "passive" iterator
    generic
        with procedure PROCESS (ELEMENT  : in out ELEMENTS;
                                CONTINUE :    out BOOLEAN);
    procedure ITERATE (LIST : in LISTS);
    -- an "active" iterator involves exporting operations like
    -- INITIATE_ITERATOR, MORE_ELEMENTS, NEXT_ELEMENT,
    -- TERMINATE_ITERATOR
    -------------------------------------------------------------
private
    type LIST_BLOCKS; -- deferred to package body
    type LISTS is access LIST_BLOCKS;
end LIST_MANAGER;
-------------------------------------------------------------------
with LIST_MANAGER;
procedure LIST_USER is
    ...
    type EMPLOYEES is ...
```

```
------------------------------------------------------------------
package MY_LIST_MANAGER is new LIST_MANAGER (ELEMENTS => EMPLOYEES);
------------------------------------------------------------------

EMPLOYEE_LIST : MY_LIST_MANAGER.LISTS;


------------------------------------------------------------------
procedure PRINT_EMPLOYEE_INFO (EMPLOYEE : in out EMPLOYEES;
                               CONTINUE :    out BOOLEAN) is
begin -- PRINT_EMPLOYEE_INFO
   -- print employee name and id.
   CONTINUE := TRUE; -- don't stop iterating here
end PRINT_EMPLOYEE_INFO;
------------------------------------------------------------------

   -- This instantiates a passive iterator that calls
   -- PRINT_EMPLOYEE_INFO once for each element.
procedure PRINT_EMPLOYEE_REPORT is new
   MY_LIST_MANAGER.ITERATE (PROCESS => PRINT_EMPLOYEE_INFO);
------------------------------------------------------------------
begin -- LIST_USER
   -- call the instantiated iterator.
   PRINT_EMPLOYEE_REPORT (EMPLOYEE_LIST);
end LIST_USER;
------------------------------------------------------------------
```

rationale

Iteration over complex data structures is often required and, if not provided by the part itself, can be difficult to implement without violating information hiding principles.

note

The example shows a passive iterator (for further discussion see [22]). For an extended discussion, including examples of both active and passive iterators, see Booch [5].

8.3.6   Part Families

guideline

• Create families of generic or other parts with similar specifications.

example

The Booch parts [5] are an excellent example of the application of this guideline.

rationale

Different versions of similar parts (e.g. bounded versus unbounded stacks) may be needed for different applications or to change the properties of a given application. Often, the different behaviors required by these versions cannot be obtained using generic parameters. Providing a family of parts with similar specifications makes it easy for the programmer to select the appropriate one for the current application, or to substitute a different one if the needs of the application change.

note

A reusable part which is structured from subparts which are members of part families is particularly easy to tailor to the needs of a given application by substitution of family members.

8.3.7   Extending Subprograms

guideline

- When adapting a subprogram by extending its functionality, provide default values for any new parameters.

rationale

See Guideline 5.2.3.

8.3.8   Symbolic Constants

guideline

- Use symbolic constants and constant expressions to allow multiple dependencies to be linked to a single or a small number of symbols.

example

```
procedure DISK_DRIVER is
    --In this procedure, a number of important disk parameters are linked.
    NUMBER_SECTORS      : constant := 4;
    NUMBER_TRACKS       : constant := 200;
    NUMBER_SURFACES     : constant := 18;
    SECTOR_CAPACITY     : constant := 4096;
    TRACK_CAPACITY      : constant := NUMBER_SECTORS  * SECTOR_CAPACITY;
    SURFACE_CAPACITY    : constant := NUMBER_TRACKS   * TRACK_CAPACITY;
    DISK_CAPACITY       : constant := NUMBER_SURFACES * SURFACE_CAPACITY;

    type SECTOR_RANGE    is range 1 .. NUMBER_SECTORS;
    type TRACK_RANGE     is range 1 .. NUMBER_TRACKS;
    type SURFACE_RANGE   is range 1 .. NUMBER_SURFACES;

    type TRACK_MAP       is array (SECTOR_RANGE) of ...;
    type SURFACE_MAP     is array (TRACK_RANGE) of TRACK_MAP;
    type DISK_MAP        is array (SURFACE_RANGE) of SURFACE_MAP;

begin
    ...
end DISK_DRIVER;
```

rationale

In order to reuse software that uses symbolic constants and constant expressions appropriately, just one or a small number of constants need to be reset and all declarations and associated code are changed automatically. Apart from easing reuse, this reduces the number of opportunities for error.

8.3.9   Unconstrained Arrays

guideline

- Make the size of local variables depend on actual parameter size where appropriate.

example

```
type VECTOR is
  array(VECTOR_INDEX range <>) of ELEMENT;
type MATRIX is
  array(VECTOR_INDEX range <>, VECTOR_INDEX range <>) of ELEMENT;
...
---------------------------------------------------------------------
procedure MATRIX_OPERATION(SUBJECT_DATA : MATRIX) is
    WORKSPACE   : MATRIX(SUBJECT_DATA'RANGE(1), SUBJECT_DATA'RANGE(2));
    TEMP_VECTOR : VECTOR(SUBJECT_DATA'FIRST(1) .. 2 * SUBJECT_DATA'LAST(1));
```

rational

Unconstrained arrays can be declared with their sizes dependent on formal parameter sizes. When used as local variables, their sizes change automatically with the supplied actual parameters. This facility can be used to assist in the adaption of a part since necessary size changes in local variables are taken care of automatically.

exception

Although this is a powerful mechanism in support of reuse, unconstrained arrays can slow procedure calls significantly because size computation takes place at run time. If run-time efficiency is a major concern, this guideline might not be used. Naturally, if this is done, it must be well documented as must the required sizes of the local variables.

8.3.10   Conditional Compilation

guideline

- Structure reusable code to exploit dead code removal by the compiler where it is supported by the implementation.

example

```
          separate(MATRIX_MATH)
     procedure INVERT( ... ) is
          type ALGORITHM is (GAUSSIAN, PIVOTING, CHOLESKI, TRI_DIAGONAL);
          WHICH_ALGORITHM : constant ALGORITHM := CHOLESKI;
     begin -- INVERT
          case WHICH_ALGORITHM is
               when GAUSSIAN     => ... ;
               when PIVOTING     => ... ;
               when CHOLESKI     => ... ;
               when TRI_DIAGONAL => ... ;
          end case;
     end INVERT;
```

rationale

Some compilers omit object code corresponding to parts of the program that they can detect will never be executed. Constant expressions in conditional statements take advantage of this feature where it is available, providing a limited form of conditional compilation. When a part is reused in an implementation that does not support this form of conditional compilation, this practice produces a clean structure which is easy to adapt by deleting or commenting out redundant code where it creates an unacceptable overhead.

caution

Be aware of whether your implementation supports dead code removal, and be prepared to take other steps to eliminate the overhead of redundant code if necessary.

8.3.11   Table Driven Programming

guideline

- Write table–driven reusable parts where possible and appropriate.

example

The epitome of table driven reusable software is a parser generation system. A specification of the form of the input data and of its output, along with some specialization code, is converted to tables that are to be "walked" by pre-existing code using predetermined algorithms in the parser produced. Other forms of "application generators" work similarly.

rationale

Table–driven (sometimes known as data–driven) programs have behavior that depends on data with'ed at compile time or read from a file at run time. In appropriate circumstances, table–driven programming provides a very powerful way of creating general purpose, easily tailorable, reusable parts.

note

Consider whether differences in the behavior of a general purpose part could be defined by some data structure at compile or run–time, and if so structure the part to be table driven. The approach is most likely to be applicable when a part is designed for use in a particular application domain but needs to be specialized for use in a specific application within the domain. Take particular care in documenting the structure of the data needed to drive the part.

8.3.12   Exceptions

guideline

- Propagate exceptions out of reusable parts. Handle exceptions within reusable parts only when you are certain that the handling will always be appropriate.

example

See example in Guideline 8.1.4.

rationale

On most occasions, an exception is raised because an undesired event (such as floating–point overflow) has occurred. Such events often need to be dealt with entirely differently with different uses of a particular software part. It is very difficult to anticipate all the ways that users of the part may wish to have the exceptions handled. Passing the exception out of the part is the safest treatment.

8.4   SUMMARY

general considerations

- Exploit the features of the Ada language to write general purpose, adaptable code that has the maximum potential for future reuse.

- Consider reusing existing software in preference to writing new code.

- Prefer reusing large parts to small.

- Consider upgrading or adapting unsuitable, e.g., non–portable, code if no appropriate reusable part is available.

- If you adapt or upgrade an existing part to reuse it, ensure that the adapted part is suitable for future reuse.

- Code reusable parts to be robust in any context.

understanding and clarity

- Document what a reusable part does.
- Document how to use it.
- Document assumptions made by the part.
- Document features of the part that are likely to change.
- Select application–independent names for reusable parts and their identifiers.
- Do not use <u>any</u> abbreviations in identifier or unit names.

adaptability

- Provide complete functionality in a reusable part or set of parts. Build in complete functionality, including end conditions, even if some functions are not needed in this application.
- Make every unit that you write a generic unit if its reuse is even a remote possibility.
- Anticipate change, and use generic parameters to facilitate adaption of generic units.
- Exploit Ada's generic construct to create readily adaptable parts that can be instantiated to operate on different types of data.
- Exploit Ada's generic construct to create readily adaptable parts that can be instantiated to provide specific functionality using generic subprogram parameters.
- Provide iterators for traversing complex data structures within reusable parts.
- Create families of generic or other parts with similar specifications.
- When adapting a subprogram by extending its functionality, provide default values for any new parameters.
- Use symbolic constants and constant expressions to allow multiple dependencies to be linked to a single or a small number of symbols.
- Make the size of local variables depend on actual parameter size where appropriate.
- Structure reusable code to exploit dead code removal by the compiler where it is supported by the implementation.
- Write table–driven reusable parts where possible and appropriate.
- Propagate exceptions out of reusable parts. Handle exceptions within reusable parts only when you are certain that the handling will always be appropriate.

Chapter 9

Instantiation

A number of guidelines in this book are generic in nature. That is, they present a general principle of good Ada style, such as consistent indentation of source text, but do not prescribe a particular instantiation of that principle. In order to allow this book to function as a coding standard, you will need a particular instantiation.

This chapter lists all the guidelines requiring instantiation, and shows the instantiation adopted for the examples in this book. You might want to consider this instantiation as a coding standard. A code formatter can enforce many of these standards or change code to meet them as needed.

9.1   HORIZONTAL SPACING

guideline (2.1.1)

- Employ a consistent spacing strategy around delimiters.

instantiation

- Employ at least one blank before and after the following delimiters: `&` `*` `+` `/` `:` `<` `=` `>` `|` `=>` `..` `:=` `/=` `>=` `<=` `<<` `>>` `<>` and `-` used as a binary operator.
- Precede the minus sign used as a unary operator by at least one blank.
- Do not leave spaces before or after `'` `.` `**` unless involved in a line break.

- Except when in conflict with other parts of this instantiation, leave at least one blank on the non–literal side of ´ and " when they delimit a character and a string literal, respectively.

- Do not leave spaces before or after parentheses which delimit argument lists or array indices.

- Where parentheses delimit an expression, leave at least one blank before the left parenthesis and after the right parenthesis, but not between multiple left or multiple right parentheses.

- Leave one blank before and after a short (1 character) identifier or literal within parentheses.

- Leave at least one blank after but no space before ; and , even if they follow a right parenthesis.

9.2   INDENTATION

guideline (2.1.2)

- Indent and align nested control structures, continuation lines, and embedded units consistently.

- Distinguish between indentation for statement–list structure and for continuation lines.

- Use a series of spaces for indentation, not the tab character.

instantiation

- Use the recommended paragraphing shown in the Ada LRM [28].

- Use 3 blanks as the basic step for indentation.

- Use 2 blanks as the basic step for indenting continuation lines.

A label is exdented 3 spaces. A continuation line is indented 2 spaces:

```
<<label>>                        |<long statement requiring line break>
   <statement>                   |  <trailing part of same statement>
```

The if statement and the plain loop:

```
if <condition> then              | <name>:
   <statements>                  |    loop
elsif <condition> then           |       <statements>
   <statements>                  |       exit when <condition>;
else                             |       <statements>
   <statements>                  |    end loop;
end if;                          |
```

Loops with the for and while iteration schemes:

```
<name>:                        | <name>:
   for <scheme> loop           |    while <condition> loop
      <statements>             |       <statements>
   end loop;                   |    end loop;
```

The block and the case statement as recommended in the Ada LRM [28]:

```
<name>:                        | case <expression> is
   declare                     |    when <choice> =>
      <declarations>           |       <statements>
   begin                       |    when <choice> =>
      <statements>             |       <statements>
   exception                   |    when others =>
      when <choice> =>         |       <statements>
         <statements>          | end case;
      when others =>           |
         <statements>          |
   end <name>;                 |
```

These case statements save space over the Ada LRM recommendation and depend on very short statement lists, respectively. Whichever you choose, be consistent.

```
case <expression> is           | case <expression> is
when <choice> =>               |    when <choice> => <statements>
      <statements>             |                     <statements>
when <choice> =>               |    when <choice> => <statements>
      <statements>             |    when others    => <statements>
when others =>                 | end case;
      <statements>             |
end case;                      |
```

The various forms of selective wait and the timed and conditional entry calls:

```
select                         | select
   when <guard> =>             |    <entry call>;
      <accept statement>       |    <statements>
      <statements>             | or
or                             |    delay <interval>;
      <accept statement>       |    <statements>
      <statements>             | end select;
or                             |
   when <guard> =>             |
      delay <interval>;        |
      <statements>             |
or                             | select
   when <guard> =>             |    <enter call>;
      terminate;               |    <statements>
else                           | else
   <statements>                |    <statements>
end select;                    | end select;
```

The accept statement and a subunit:

```
accept <specification> do            |    separate(<parent unit>)
   <statements>                      | <proper body>
end <name>;                          |
```

Body stubs of the program units:

```
procedure <specification> is         | package body <name> is
   separate;                         |    separate;
                                     |
function <specification>             | task body <name> is
  return <type> is                   |    separate;
   separate;                         |
```

Proper bodies of program units:

```
procedure <specification> is         | package body <name> is
   <declarations>                    |    <declarations>
begin                                | begin
   <statements>                      |    <statements>
exception                            | exception
   when <choice> =>                  |    when <choice> =>
      <statements>                   |       <statements>
end <name>;                          | end <name>;
                                     |
function <specification>             | task body <name> is
  return <type name> is              |    <declarations>
   <declarations>                    | begin
begin                                |    <statements>
   <statements>                      | exception
exception                            |    when <choice> =>
   when <choice> =>                  |       <statements>
      <statements>                   | end <name>;
end <name>;                          |
```

Context clauses on compilation units are arranged as a table, and are indented so as not to obscure the introductory line of the unit itself. Generic formal parameters do not obscure the unit itself. Function, package, and task specifications use standard indent:

```
with <name>,                         |function <specification>
     <name>,                         |   return <type>;
     <name>;                         |
use  <name>,                         |package <name> is
     <name>,                         |   <declarations>
     <name>;                         |private
<compilation unit>                   |   <declarations>
                                     |end <name>;
                                     |
generic -- <kind of unit> <name>     |task type <name> is
   <formal parameters>               |   entry <declaration>
<compilation unit>                   |end <name>;
```

Instantiations of generic units, and indentation of a record:

```
procedure <name> is                    | type ... is
   new <generic name> <actuals>        |    record
                                        |       <component list>
function <name> is                      |       case <discriminant name> is
   new <generic name> <actuals>         |          when <choice> =>
                                        |             <component list>
package <name> is                       |          when <choice> =>
   new <generic name> <actuals>         |             <component list>
                                        |       end case;
                                        | end record;
```

Indentation for record alignment:

```
for <name> use
   record <alignment clause>
      <component clause>
   end record;
```

9.3 MORE ON ALIGNMENT

guideline (2.1.5)

- Align parameter modes and grouping symbols vertically.

- Use four trailing blanks for mode in and three leading blanks for mode out.

instantiation

- Place one formal parameter specification per line.

- Vertically align parameter names; vertically align colons; vertically align the reserved word in; vertically align the reserved word out; vertically align parameter types.

- Place the first parameter specification on the same line as the subprogram or entry name. If any of the parameter types are forced beyond the line length limit, place the first parameter specification on a new line indented as for continuation lines.

The following two subprogram specifications adhere to this rule:

```
procedure DISPLAY_MENU (TITLE   : in    STRING;
                        OPTIONS : in    MENUS;
                        CHOICE  :    out ALPHA_NUMERICS);
```

or

```
procedure DISPLAY_MENU_ON_PRIMARY_WINDOW
   (TITLE   : in    STRING;
    OPTIONS : in    MENUS;
    CHOICE  :    out ALPHA_NUMERICS);
```

9.4   PAGINATION

guideline (2.1.7)

- Mark the top of the body of each program unit and the beginning and end of its frame.
- Mark the top and bottom of a package specification.

instantiation

- Use a line of dashes to the end of the line, beginning at the same column as the current indentation.
- If two dashed lines would be adjacent, use only the shorter of the two.
- If there are no more than two one-line declarations within a unit, the dashed line above the begin can be omitted.
- A line precedes, but does not separate the context clauses preceding the reserved words package, generic, procedure, function from those reserved words.

9.5   SOURCE CODE LINE LENGTH

guideline (2.1.9)

- Adhere to a maximum line length limit for source code.

instantiation

- Limit source code line lengths to a maximum of 72 characters.

9.6   NUMBERS

guideline (3.1.2)

- Represent numbers in a consistent fashion.
- Use an appropriate base for literals.
- Use underscores to separate digits the same way commas would be used in handwritten text.
- When using Scientific notation, make the "e" consistently either upper or lower case.
- In an alternate base, represent the alphabetic characters in either all upper case, or all lower case.

- Use underscores in alternate base numbers in the same way blanks or commas would be used in handwritten text.

instantiation

- Decimal and octal numbers are grouped by threes beginning counting on either side of the radix point.
- The "ᴇ" is always capitalized in scientific notation.
- Use all capitals for the alphabetic characters representing digits in bases above 10.
- Hexadecimal numbers are grouped by fours beginning counting on either side of the radix point.

9.7   CAPITALIZATION

guideline (3.1.3)

- Make reserved words and other elements of the program distinct from each other.

instantiation

- Use lower case letters for all reserved words.
- Use upper case for all other identifiers.

9.8   FILE HEADERS

guideline (3.2.2)

- Place in the header of Ada source code only information that will identify important characteristics of the code.
- Include in header comments only what a reader will trust.
- Include copyright notices.
- Include author name(s), dates, and place.
- Indicate where to look for implementation and machine dependencies.

instantiation

The following information is to be placed in file headers:

- names of the authors of the code,
- the dates of creation and of the most recent change to the code,

- the authors' department(s) within the organization, and the organization, if the code is released outside without a copyright notice,

- a copyright notice, if required,

- a three–line–maximum description of the location of each implementation– or machine dependency, unless the file serves to isolate such dependencies.

A template for file headers used in this book follows:

```
------------------------------------------------------------------------
-- Author:
-- Date:
-- Department:
-- Copyright:
-- Dependencies:
------------------------------------------------------------------------
```

9.9 NAMED ASSOCIATION

guideline (5.2.2)

- Use named parameter association in calls of infrequently used subprograms or entries with many formal parameters.

- Use named component association for constants, expressions, and literals in aggregate initializations.

- Use named association when instantiating generics with many formal parameters.

- Use named association for clarification when the actual parameter is TRUE or FALSE or an expression.

- Use named association when supplying a non–default value to an optional parameter.

instantiation

- Use named parameter association in calls of subprograms or entries called from less than 5 places or with more than 4 formal parameters.

- Use named association when instantiating generics with more than 4 formal parameters.

9.10 ORDER OF PARAMETER DECLARATIONS

guideline (5.2.5)

- Declare parameters in a consistent order.

instantiation

- All required in parameters are declared before any in out parameter.
- All in out parameters are declared before any out parameters.
- All out parameters are declared before any optional parameters
- The order of parameters within these groups is derived from the needs of the application.

9.11 NESTING

guideline (5.6.1)

- Restrict or minimize the depth of nested expressions and control structures.
- Try simplification heuristics.

instantiation

- Do not nest expressions or control structures beyond a nesting level of 5.

9.12 GLOBAL ASSUMPTIONS

guideline (7.1.1)

- Make considered assumptions about the support an implementation will provide for the following:
  - Number of bits available for type INTEGER.
  - Number of decimal digits of precision available for floating point types.
  - Number of bits available for fixed–point types.
  - Number of characters per line of source text.
  - Number of bits for *universal_integer* expressions.
  - Number of seconds for the range of DURATION.
  - Number of milliseconds for DURATION′SMALL.

instantiation

These are minimum values (or minimum precision in the case of DURATION′SMALL) that an implementation must provide. There is no guarantee that a given implementation will provide more than the minimum, so these should be treated as maximum values also.

- 16 bits available for type INTEGER.

- 6 decimal digits of precision available for floating point types.
- 32 bits available for fixed–point types.
- 72 characters per line of source text.
- 16 bits for *universal_integer* expressions.
- –86_400 .. 86_400 seconds (1 day) for the range of DURATION.
- 20 milliseconds for DURATION′SMALL.

Chapter 10

Complete Example

This chapter contains an example program to illustrate use of the guidelines. The program implements a simple menu–driven user interface that could be used as the front end for a variety of applications. It consists of a package for locally defined types (SPC_NUMERIC_TYPES), instantiations of I/O packages for those types (found in **spc_int_io_.a** and **spc_real_io_.a**), a package to perform Ascii terminal I/O for generating menus, writing prompts and receiving user input (TERMINAL_IO), and finally an example using the terminal I/O routines (EXAMPLE).

Within TERMINAL_IO, subprogram names are overloaded when several subprograms perform the same general function but for different data types.

The body for TERMINAL_IO uses separate compilation capabilities for a subprogram, DISPLAY_MENU, that is larger and more involved than the rest. Note that all literals that would be required are defined as constants. Nested loops, where they exist, are also named. The function defined in the file **terminal_io.a** on line 63 encapsulates a local exception handler within a loop. Where locally defined types could not be used, there is a comment explaining the reason. The use of short circuit control forms, both on an if statement and an exit are also illustrated.

The information that would have been in the file headers is redundant since it is contained in the title page of this book. The file headers are omitted from the following listings.

FILE: numerics_.a

```
 1:----------------------------------------------------------------
 2:package SPC_NUMERIC_TYPES is
 3:
 4:    type TINY_INTEGER   is range -(2**7)  .. (2**7)  - 1;
 5:
 6:    type MEDIUM_INTEGER is range -(2**15) .. (2**15) - 1;
 7:
 8:    type BIG_INTEGER    is range -(2**31) .. (2**31) - 1;
 9:
10:    subtype TINY_NATURAL
11:      is TINY_INTEGER    range 0 .. TINY_INTEGER'LAST;
12:
13:    subtype MEDIUM_NATURAL
14:      is MEDIUM_INTEGER range 0 .. MEDIUM_INTEGER'LAST;
15:
16:    subtype BIG_NATURAL
17:      is BIG_INTEGER     range 0 .. BIG_INTEGER'LAST;
18:
19:    subtype TINY_POSITIVE
20:      is TINY_INTEGER    range 1 .. TINY_INTEGER'LAST;
21:
22:    subtype MEDIUM_POSITIVE
23:      is MEDIUM_INTEGER range 1 .. MEDIUM_INTEGER'LAST;
24:
25:    subtype BIG_POSITIVE
26:      is BIG_INTEGER     range 1 .. BIG_INTEGER'LAST;
27:
28:    type MEDIUM_FLOAT is digits 6;
29:    type BIG_FLOAT    is digits 9;
30:
31:    subtype PROBABILITIES is MEDIUM_FLOAT   range 0.0 .. 1.0;
32:
33:    ----------------------------------------------------------------
34:    function MIN (LEFT  : in TINY_INTEGER;
35:                  RIGHT : in TINY_INTEGER)
36:      return TINY_INTEGER;
37:    ----------------------------------------------------------------
38:    function MAX (LEFT  : in TINY_INTEGER;
39:                  RIGHT : in TINY_INTEGER)
40:      return TINY_INTEGER;
41:    ----------------------------------------------------------------
42:    -- Additional function declarations
43:    -- to return the minimum and maximum values for each type.
44:end SPC_NUMERIC_TYPES;
45:----------------------------------------------------------------
```

FILE: numerics.a

```
 1:----------------------------------------------------------------
 2:package body SPC_NUMERIC_TYPES is
 3:
 4:    ------------------------------------------------------------
 5:    function MIN (LEFT  : in TINY_INTEGER;
 6:                  RIGHT : in TINY_INTEGER)
 7:      return TINY_INTEGER is
 8:    begin -- MIN
 9:      if LEFT < RIGHT then
10:         return LEFT;
11:      else
12:         return RIGHT;
13:      end if;
14:    end MIN;
15:    ------------------------------------------------------------
16:    function MAX (LEFT  : in TINY_INTEGER;
17:                  RIGHT : in TINY_INTEGER)
18:      return TINY_INTEGER is
19:
20:    begin -- MAX
21:      if LEFT > RIGHT then
22:         return LEFT;
23:      else
24:         return RIGHT;
25:      end if;
26:    end MAX;
27:    ------------------------------------------------------------
28:    -- Additional functions to return minimum and maximum
29:    -- value for each type defined in the package.
30:    ------------------------------------------------------------
31:end SPC_NUMERIC_TYPES;
32:----------------------------------------------------------------
```

FILE: spc_int_io_.a

```
 1:----------------------------------------------------------------
 2:with SPC_NUMERIC_TYPES,
 3:     TEXT_IO;
 4:package SPC_SMALL_INTEGER_IO is new
 5:  TEXT_IO.INTEGER_IO (SPC_NUMERIC_TYPES.TINY_INTEGER);
 6:----------------------------------------------------------------
 7:with SPC_NUMERIC_TYPES,
 8:     TEXT_IO;
 9:package MEDIUM_INTEGER_IO is new
10:  TEXT_IO.INTEGER_IO (SPC_NUMERIC_TYPES.MEDIUM_INTEGER);
11:----------------------------------------------------------------
12:with SPC_NUMERIC_TYPES,
13:     TEXT_IO;
14:package BIG_INTEGER_IO is new
15:  TEXT_IO.INTEGER_IO (SPC_NUMERIC_TYPES.BIG_INTEGER);
16:----------------------------------------------------------------
```

FILE: spc_real_io_.a

```
 1:-------------------------------------------------------------
 2:with SPC_NUMERIC_TYPES,
 3:     TEXT_IO;
 4:package MEDIUM_FLOAT_IO is new
 5:  TEXT_IO.FLOAT_IO (SPC_NUMERIC_TYPES.MEDIUM_FLOAT);
 6:-------------------------------------------------------------
 7:with SPC_NUMERIC_TYPES,
 8:     TEXT_IO;
 9:package BIG_FLOAT_IO is new
10:  TEXT_IO.FLOAT_IO (SPC_NUMERIC_TYPES.BIG_FLOAT);
11:-------------------------------------------------------------
```

FILE: terminal_io_.a

```
 1:-------------------------------------------------------------
 2:with SPC_NUMERIC_TYPES;
 3:use  SPC_NUMERIC_TYPES;
 4:
 5:package TERMINAL_IO is
 6:
 7:   MAX_FILE_NAME : constant := 30;
 8:   MAX_LINE      : constant := 30;
 9:
10:   subtype ALPHA_NUMERICS is CHARACTER range '0' .. 'Z';
11:   subtype LINES is STRING (1 .. MAX_LINE);
12:
13:   EMPTY_LINE : constant LINES := (others => ' ');
14:
15:   type MENUS is array (ALPHA_NUMERICS) of LINES;
16:
17:   subtype FILE_NAMES is STRING (1 .. MAX_FILE_NAME);
18:   ----------------------------------------------------------
19:   procedure GET_FILE_NAME (PROMPT      : in     STRING;
20:                            NAME        :    out FILE_NAMES;
21:                            NAME_LENGTH :    out NATURAL);
22:   ----------------------------------------------------------
23:   function YES (PROMPT : STRING) return BOOLEAN;
24:   ----------------------------------------------------------
25:   function GET (PROMPT : STRING) return MEDIUM_INTEGER;
26:   ----------------------------------------------------------
27:   function GET (PROMPT : STRING) return MEDIUM_FLOAT;
28:   ----------------------------------------------------------
29:   procedure DISPLAY_MENU (TITLE   : in     STRING;
30:                           OPTIONS : in     MENUS;
31:                           CHOICE  :    out ALPHA_NUMERICS);
32:   ----------------------------------------------------------
33:   procedure PAUSE (PROMPT : STRING);
34:   ----------------------------------------------------------
35:   procedure PAUSE;
36:   ----------------------------------------------------------
37:   procedure PUT (INTEGER_VALUE : MEDIUM_INTEGER);
38:   ----------------------------------------------------------
39:   procedure PUT (REAL_VALUE : MEDIUM_FLOAT);
```

```
40:      ----------------------------------------------------------
41:      procedure PUT (LABEL           : STRING;
42:                     INTEGER_VALUE : MEDIUM_INTEGER);
43:      ----------------------------------------------------------
44:      procedure PUT (LABEL           : STRING;
45:                     REAL_VALUE : MEDIUM_FLOAT);
46:      ----------------------------------------------------------
47:      procedure PUT_LINE (INTEGER_VALUE : MEDIUM_INTEGER);
48:      ----------------------------------------------------------
49:      procedure PUT_LINE (REAL_VALUE : MEDIUM_FLOAT);
50:      ----------------------------------------------------------
51:      procedure PUT_LINE (LABEL           : STRING;
52:                          INTEGER_VALUE : MEDIUM_INTEGER);
53:      ----------------------------------------------------------
54:      procedure PUT_LINE (LABEL           : STRING;
55:                          REAL_VALUE : MEDIUM_FLOAT);
56:      ----------------------------------------------------------
57:end TERMINAL_IO;
58:----------------------------------------------------------------
```

FILE: terminal_io.a

```
 1:----------------------------------------------------------------
 2:with MEDIUM_INTEGER_IO,
 3:     MEDIUM_FLOAT_IO,
 4:     TEXT_IO;
 5:
 6:use  TEXT_IO;
 7:
 8:package body TERMINAL_IO is   -- simple terminal i/o routines
 9:
10:     subtype RESPONSE is STRING (1 .. 20);
11:
12:     PROMPT_COLUMN     : constant                := 30;
13:     QUESTION_MARK     : constant STRING    := " ? ";
14:     STANDARD_PROMPT : constant STRING    := " ==> ";
15:     BLANK             : constant CHARACTER := ' ';
16:     --------------------------------------------------------
17:     procedure PUT_PROMPT (PROMPT    : STRING;
18:                           QUESTION : BOOLEAN := FALSE) is
19:     begin -- PUT_PROMPT
20:        PUT(PROMPT);
21:        if QUESTION then
22:           PUT(QUESTION_MARK);
23:        end if;
24:        SET_COL(PROMPT_COLUMN);
25:        PUT(STANDARD_PROMPT);
26:     end PUT_PROMPT;
27:     --------------------------------------------------------
28:     function YES (PROMPT : STRING) return BOOLEAN is
29:
30:        RESPONSE_STRING              : RESPONSE := (others => BLANK);
31:        RESPONSE_STRING_LENGTH : NATURAL;
32:        --------------------------------------------------------
33:     begin -- YES
```

```
34:        GET_RESPONSE:
35:        loop
36:           PUT_PROMPT(PROMPT, QUESTION => TRUE);
37:           GET_LINE(RESPONSE_STRING, RESPONSE_STRING_LENGTH);
38:           for POSITION in 1 .. RESPONSE_STRING_LENGTH loop
39:              if RESPONSE_STRING(POSITION) /= BLANK then
40:                 return ((RESPONSE_STRING(POSITION) = 'Y') or
41:                         (RESPONSE_STRING(POSITION) = 'y'));
42:              end if;
43:           end loop;
44:           NEW_LINE; -- issue prompt until non-blank response
45:        end loop GET_RESPONSE;
46: end YES;
47: ------------------------------------------------------------
48: procedure GET_FILE_NAME
49:    (PROMPT      : in     STRING;
50:     NAME        :    out FILE_NAMES;
51:     NAME_LENGTH :    out NATURAL) is
52: begin -- GET_FILE_NAME
53:    PUT_PROMPT(PROMPT);
54:    GET_LINE(NAME, NAME_LENGTH);
55: end GET_FILE_NAME;
56: ------------------------------------------------------------
57: function GET (PROMPT : STRING) return MEDIUM_INTEGER is
58:
59:    RESPONSE_STRING: RESPONSE := (others => BLANK);
60:    LAST           : NATURAL; -- Required by GET_LINE.
61:    VALUE          : MEDIUM_INTEGER;
62:    --------------------------------------------------------
63: begin -- GET
64:    loop
65:       begin
66:          PUT_PROMPT(PROMPT);
67:          GET_LINE(RESPONSE_STRING, LAST);
68:          VALUE:=
69:             MEDIUM_INTEGER'VALUE(RESPONSE_STRING(1.. LAST));
70:          return VALUE;
71:       exception
72:          when others =>
73              PUT_LINE("Please enter an integer");
74:       end;
75:    end loop;
76: end GET;
77: ------------------------------------------------------------
78: procedure DISPLAY_MENU (TITLE   : in     STRING;
79:                         OPTIONS : in     MENUS;
80:                         CHOICE  :    out ALPHA_NUMERICS)
81:    is separate;
82: ------------------------------------------------------------
83: procedure PAUSE (PROMPT: STRING) is
84: begin -- PAUSE
85:    PUT_LINE(PROMPT);
86:    PAUSE;
87: end PAUSE;
88: ------------------------------------------------------------
```

```
89:    procedure PAUSE is
90:       BUFFER : RESPONSE;
91:       LAST   : NATURAL;
92:    begin -- pause
93:       PUT("Press return to continue");
94:       GET_LINE(BUFFER, LAST);
95:    end PAUSE;
96:    ------------------------------------------------------------
97:    function GET (PROMPT : STRING) return MEDIUM_FLOAT is
98:
99:       VALUE: MEDIUM_FLOAT;
100:      ------------------------------------------------------------
101:   begin -- GET
102:      loop
103:         begin
104:            PUT_PROMPT(PROMPT);
105:            MEDIUM_FLOAT_IO.GET(VALUE);
106:            SKIP_LINE;
107:            return VALUE;
108:         exception
109:            when others =>
110:               SKIP_LINE;
111:               PUT_LINE("Please enter a real number");
112:         end;
113:      end loop;
114:   end GET;
115:   ------------------------------------------------------------
116:   procedure PUT (INTEGER_VALUE : MEDIUM_INTEGER) is
117:   begin -- PUT
118:      MEDIUM_INTEGER_IO.PUT(INTEGER_VALUE, WIDTH => 4);
119:   end PUT;
120:   ------------------------------------------------------------
121:   procedure PUT (REAL_VALUE : MEDIUM_FLOAT) is
122:   begin -- PUT
123:      MEDIUM_FLOAT_IO.PUT(REAL_VALUE, FORE => 4,  AFT => 3,
124:         EXP => 0);
125:   end PUT;
126:   ------------------------------------------------------------
127:   procedure PUT (LABEL         : STRING;
128:                  INTEGER_VALUE : MEDIUM_INTEGER) is
129:   begin -- PUT
130:      TEXT_IO.PUT(LABEL);
131:      MEDIUM_INTEGER_IO.PUT(INTEGER_VALUE);
132:   end PUT;
133:   ------------------------------------------------------------
134:   procedure PUT (LABEL      : STRING;
135:                  REAL_VALUE : MEDIUM_FLOAT) is
136:   begin -- PUT
137:      TEXT_IO.PUT(LABEL);
138:      MEDIUM_FLOAT_IO.PUT(REAL_VALUE, FORE => 4, AFT => 3,
139:         EXP => 0);
140:   end PUT;
141:   ------------------------------------------------------------
142:   procedure PUT_LINE (INTEGER_VALUE : MEDIUM_INTEGER) is
143:   begin -- PUT_LINE
```

```
144:        TERMINAL_IO.PUT(INTEGER_VALUE);
145:        TEXT_IO.NEW_LINE;
146:     end PUT_LINE;
147:     ------------------------------------------------------------
148:     procedure PUT_LINE (REAL_VALUE : MEDIUM_FLOAT) is
149:     begin -- PUT_LINE
150:        TERMINAL_IO.PUT(REAL_VALUE);
151:        TEXT_IO.NEW_LINE;
152:     end PUT_LINE;
153:     ------------------------------------------------------------
154:     procedure PUT_LINE (LABEL         : STRING;
155:                         INTEGER_VALUE : MEDIUM_INTEGER) is
156:     begin -- PUT_LINE
157:        TERMINAL_IO.PUT(LABEL, INTEGER_VALUE);
158:        TEXT_IO.NEW_LINE;
159:     end PUT_LINE;
160:     ------------------------------------------------------------
161:     procedure PUT_LINE (LABEL         : STRING;
162:                         REAL_VALUE : MEDIUM_FLOAT) is
163:     begin -- PUT_LINE
164:        TERMINAL_IO.PUT(LABEL, REAL_VALUE);
165:        TEXT_IO.NEW_LINE;
166:     end PUT_LINE;
167:     ------------------------------------------------------------
168:
169: end TERMINAL_IO;
170: ------------------------------------------------------------
```

FILE: terminal_io__display_menu.a

```
 1: ------------------------------------------------------------
 2: separate (TERMINAL_IO)
 3: procedure DISPLAY_MENU (TITLE   : in      STRING;
 4:                         OPTIONS : in      MENUS;
 5:                         CHOICE  :     out ALPHA_NUMERICS) is
 6:
 7:    LEFT_COLUMN  : constant        := 15;
 8:    RIGHT_COLUMN : constant        := 20;
 9:    PROMPT       : constant STRING := " ==> ";
10:
11:    type ALPHA_ARRAY is array (ALPHA_NUMERICS) of BOOLEAN;
12:
13:    VALID        : BOOLEAN;
14:    VALID_OPTION : ALPHA_ARRAY := (others => FALSE);
15:    ------------------------------------------------------------
16:    procedure DRAW_MENU (TITLE   : STRING;
17:                         OPTIONS : MENUS) is
18:    begin -- DRAW_MENU
19:       NEW_PAGE;
20:       NEW_LINE;
21:       SET_COL(RIGHT_COLUMN);
22:       PUT_LINE(TITLE);
23:       NEW_LINE;
24:       for CHOICE in ALPHA_NUMERICS loop
25:          if OPTIONS(CHOICE) /= EMPTY_LINE then
```

```
26:              VALID_OPTION(CHOICE) := TRUE;
27:              SET_COL(LEFT_COLUMN);
28:              PUT(CHOICE & " -- ");
29:              PUT_LINE(OPTIONS(CHOICE));
30:           end if;
31:        end loop;
32:    end DRAW_MENU;
33:    ------------------------------------------------------------
34:    procedure GET_RESPONSE (VALID  : out BOOLEAN;
35:                            CHOICE : out ALPHA_NUMERICS) is
36:
37:        BUFFER_SIZE : constant                  := 20;
38:        DUMMY       : constant ALPHA_NUMERICS := 'X';
39:
40:        FIRST_CHAR  : CHARACTER;
41:        BUFFER      : STRING (1 .. BUFFER_SIZE);
42:
43:        -- IMPLEMENTATION NOTE:
44:        -- The following two declarations do not use
45:        -- locally defined types because a variable of type
46:        -- NATURAL is required by the TEXT_IO routines for
47:        -- strings, and there is no relational operator defined
48:        -- for our local TINY_, MEDIUM_, or BIG_POSITIVE and
49:        -- the standard type NATURAL.
50:        LAST        : NATURAL;
51:        INDEX       : POSITIVE;
52:        ------------------------------------------------------------
53:        function UPPER_CASE (CURRENT_CHAR : CHARACTER)
54:          return CHARACTER is
55:
56:            CASE_DIFFERENCE : constant := 16#20#;
57:        ------------------------------------------------------------
58:        begin -- UPPER_CASE
59:          if CURRENT_CHAR in 'a' .. 'z' then
60:              return CHARACTER'VAL(CHARACTER'POS(CURRENT_CHAR)
61:                                    - CASE_DIFFERENCE);
62:          else
63:              return CURRENT_CHAR;
64:          end if;
65:        end UPPER_CASE;
66:        ------------------------------------------------------------
67:    begin -- GET_RESPONSE
68:
69:        NEW_LINE;
70:        SET_COL(LEFT_COLUMN);
71:        PUT(PROMPT);
72:
73:        GET_LINE(BUFFER, LAST);
74:
75:        INDEX := POSITIVE'FIRST;
76:        loop
77:          exit when  (INDEX          >= LAST              ) or else
78:                     (BUFFER(INDEX) in ALPHA_NUMERICS)           );
79:              INDEX := POSITIVE'SUCC(INDEX);
80:        end loop;
```

```
 81:
 82:          FIRST_CHAR := UPPER_CASE(BUFFER(INDEX));
 83:
 84:      if (FIRST_CHAR not in ALPHA_NUMERICS) or else
 85:         (not VALID_OPTION(FIRST_CHAR)     )          then
 86:         VALID  := FALSE;
 87:         CHOICE := DUMMY;
 88:      else
 89:         VALID  := TRUE;
 90:         CHOICE := FIRST_CHAR;
 91:      end if;
 92:
 93:  end GET_RESPONSE;
 94:  ------------------------------------------------------------
 95:  procedure BEEP is
 96:  begin
 97:     PUT(ASCII.BEL);
 98:  end BEEP;
 99:  ------------------------------------------------------------
100:begin -- DISPLAY_MENU
101:   loop
102:      DRAW_MENU(TITLE, OPTIONS);
103:      GET_RESPONSE(VALID, CHOICE);
104:      exit when VALID;
105:      BEEP;
106:   end loop;
107:end DISPLAY_MENU;
108:------------------------------------------------------------
```

FILE: example.a

```
 1:------------------------------------------------------------------
 2:with SPC_NUMERIC_TYPES,
 3:      TERMINAL_IO;
 4:------------------------------------------------------------------
 5:procedure EXAMPLE is
 6:
 7:    package TIO renames TERMINAL_IO;
 8:
 9:    EXAMPLE_MENU : constant TIO.MENUS :=
10:       TIO.MENUS'('A'     => "Add item          ",
11:                  'D'     => "Delete item       ",
12:                  'M'     => "Modify item       ",
13:                  'Q'     => "Quit              ",
14:                  others => TIO.EMPTY_LINE);
15:
16:    USER_CHOICE : TIO.ALPHA_NUMERICS;
17:    ITEM        : SPC_NUMERIC_TYPES.MEDIUM_INTEGER;
18:    ------------------------------------------------------------------
19:begin -- EXAMPLE
20:
21:    loop
22:       TIO.DISPLAY_MENU("Example Menu", EXAMPLE_MENU,
23:         USER_CHOICE);
24:
25:       case USER_CHOICE is
26:         when 'A'    =>
27:            ITEM := TIO.GET("Item to add");
28:         when 'D'    =>
29:            ITEM := TIO.GET("Item to delete");
30:         when 'M'    =>
31:            ITEM := TIO.GET("Item to modify");
32:         when 'Q'    =>
33:            exit;
34:         when others => -- error has already been
35:            null;         -- signaled to user
36:       end case;
37:
38:    end loop;
39:
40:end EXAMPLE;
41:------------------------------------------------------------------
42:
43:--  This is what is displayed, anything but A, D, M or Q beeps
44:--
45:--                  Example Menu
46:--
47:--          A -- Add item
48:--          D -- Delete item
49:--          M -- Modify item
50:--          Q -- Quit
51:--
52:--              ==>
```

Appendix A

APPENDIX A
Map from Ada Language Reference Manual to Guidelines

References

[1] ACVC (Ada Compiler Validation Capability). Ada Validation Facility, ASD/SIOL. Wright–Patterson Air Force Base, OH.

[2] Anderson, T. and R. W. Witty. 1978. Safe Programming. *BIT (Tidscrift Nordisk for Informations behandling)* 18:1–8.

[3] ARTEWG. November 5, 1986. *Catalogue of Ada Runtime Implementation Dependencies*, draft version. Association for Computing Machinery, Special Interest Group for Ada, Ada Run–Time Environments Working Group.

[4] Barnes, J. G. P. 1989. *Programming in Ada*. third edition. Reading, MA.: Addison–Wesley.

[5] Booch, G. 1987. *Software Components with Ada – Structures, Tools and Subsystems*. Menlo Park, Ca.: The Benjamin/Cummings Publishing Company, Inc.

[6] Booch, G. 1987. *Software Engineering with Ada*. second edition. Menlo Park, CA: The Benjamin/Cummings Publishing Company, Inc.

[7] Charrette, R. N. 1986. *Software Engineering Environments Concepts and Technology*. Intertext Publications Inc. New York: McGraw–Hill Inc.

[8] Cohen, N. H. 1986. *Ada as a Second Language*. New York: McGraw–Hill Inc.

[9]   Conti, R. A. March 1987. Critical Run–Time Design Tradeoffs in an Ada Implementation. *Proceedings of the Joint Ada Conference, Fifth National Conference on Ada Technology and Washington Ada Symposium.* pp. 486–495.

[10] Cristian, F. March 1984. Correct and Robust Programs. *IEEE Transactions on Software Engineering.* SE–10(2):163–174.

[11] Foreman, J. and J. Goodenough. May 1987. *Ada Adoption Handbook: A Program Manager's Guide.* Version 1.0, CMU/SEI–87–TR–9 ESD–TR–87–110. Software Engineering Institute.

[12] Goodenough, J. B. March 1986. A Sample of Ada Programmer Errors. *Unpublished draft resident in the Ada Repository under file name* PD2:<ADA.EDUCATION>PROGERRS.DOC.2.

[13] MacLaren, L. November 1980. Evolving Toward Ada in Real Time Systems. *ACM Sigplan Notices.* 15(11):146–155.

[14] Matthews, E. R. September, October 1987. Observations on the Portability of Ada I/O. *ACM Ada Letters.* VII(5):100–103.

[15] Melliar–Smith, P. M. and B. Randell. March 1987. Software Reliability: The Role of Programmed Exception Handling. *ACM Sigplan Notices.* 12(3):95–100 .

[16] Mowday, B. L. and E. Normand. November 1986. *Ada Programming Standards.* General Dynamics Data Systems Division Departmental Instruction 414.717.

[17] NASA. May 1987. *Ada Style Guide.* Version 1.1, SEL–87–002. Goddard Space Flight Center: Greenbelt, MD 20771.

[18] Nissen, J. and P. Wallis. 1984. *Portability and Style in Ada.* Cambridge University Press.

[19] Pappas, F. March 1985. *Ada Portability Guidelines.* DTIC/NTIS #AD–A160 390.

[20] Pyle, I. C. 1985. *The Ada Programming Language.* second edition. UK.: Prentice–Hall International.

[21] Rosen, J. P. November, December 1987. In Defense of the 'Use' Clause. *ACM Ada Letters.* VII(7):77–81.

[22] Ross, D. March–April 1989. The Form of a Passive Iterator. *ACM Ada Letters.* IX(2):102–105.

[23] Schneiderman, B. 1986. Empirical Studies of Programmers: The Territory, Paths and Destinations. *Empirical Studies of Programmers.* ed. E. Soloway and S. Iyengar. pp. 1–12. Norwood, NJ: Ablex Publishing Corp.

[24] Soloway, E., J. Pinto, S. Fertig, S. Letovsky, R. Lampert, D. Littman, K. Ewing. December 1986. Studying Software Documentation From A Cognitive Perspective: A Status Report. *Proceedings of the Eleventh Annual Software Engineering Workshop.* Report SEL–86–006, Software Engineering Laboratory. Greenbelt, Maryland:NASA Goddard Space Flight Center.

[25] St.Dennis, R. May 1986. *A Guidebook for Writing Reusable Source Code in Ada* –Version 1.1. Report CSC–86–3:8213. Golden Valley, Minnesota: Honeywell Corporate Systems Development Division.

[26] United Technologies. February 9, 1987. *CENC Programmer's Guide.* Appendix A Ada Programming Standards.

[27] U.S. Department of Defense, Ada Joint Program Office. 1984. *Rationale for the Design of the Ada Programming Language.*

[28] U.S. Department of Defense, Ada Joint Program Office. January 1983. *Reference Manual for the Ada Programming Language.* ANSI/MIL–STD–1815A.

[29] Volz, R. A., Mudge, Naylor and Mayer. May 1985. Some Problems in Distributing Real–time Ada Programs Across Machines. *Ada in Use, Proceedings of the Ada International Conference.* pp. 14–16. Paris.

Bibliography

ACVC (Ada Compiler Validation Capability). Ada Validation Facility, ASD/SIOL. Wright–Patterson Air Force Base, OH.

Anderson, T. and R. W. Witty. 1978. Safe Programming. *BIT* (*Tidscrift Nordisk for Informations behandling*) 18:1–8.

ARTEWG. November 5, 1986. *Catalogue of Ada Runtime Implementation Dependencies*, draft version. Association for Computing Machinery, Special Interest Group for Ada, Ada Run–Time Environments Working Group.

Bardin, Thompson. Jan–Feb 1988. Composable Ada Software Components and the Re–Export Paradigm. *ACM Ada Letters.* VIII(1):58–79.

Bardin, Thompson. March–April 1988. Using the Re–Export Paradigm to Build Composable Ada Software Components. *ACM Ada Letters.* VIII(2):39–54.

Barnes, J. G. P. 1989. *Programming in Ada.* third edition. Reading, MA.: Addison–Wesley.

Booch, G. 1987. *Software Components with Ada – Structures, Tools and Subsystems.* Menlo Park, CA.: The Benjamin/Cummings Publishing Company, Inc.

Booch, G. 1987. *Software Engineering with Ada.* second edition. Menlo Park, CA: The Benjamin/Cummings Publishing Company, Inc.

Brooks, F. B. 1975. *The Mythical Man–Month.* Essays on Software Engineering. Reading, MA:Addison–Wesley.

Charrette, R. N. 1986. *Software Engineering Environments Concepts and Technology.* Intertext Publications Inc. New York: McGraw–Hill Inc.

Cohen, N. H. 1986. *Ada as a Second Language.* New York: McGraw–Hill Inc.

Conti, R. A. March 1987. Critical Run–Time Design Tradeoffs in an Ada Implementation. *Proceedings of the Joint Ada Conference, Fifth National Conference on Ada Technology and Washington Ada Symposium.* pp. 486–495.

Cristian, F. March 1984. Correct and Robust Programs. *IEEE Transactions on Software Engineering.* SE–10(2):163–174.

Foreman, J. and J. Goodenough. May 1987. *Ada Adoption Handbook: A Program Manager's Guide.* Version 1.0, CMU/SEI–87–TR–9 ESD–TR–87–110. Software Engineering Institute.

Gary, B. and D. Pokrass. 1985, *Understanding Ada A Software Engineering Approach.* John Wiley & Sons.

Goodenough, J. B. March 1986. A Sample of Ada Programmer Errors. *Unpublished draft resident in the Ada Repository under file name* PD2:<ADA.EDUCATION>PROGERRS.DOC.2.

Herr, C. S. August 1987. Compiler Validation and Reusable Software. St. Louis: a Report from the CAMP Project, McDonnell Douglas Astronautics Company.

International Workshop on Real–Time Ada Issues. 1987. *ACM Ada Letters.* VII(6). Mortonhampstead, Devon, U.K.

International Workshop on Real–Time Ada Issues II. 1988. *ACM Ada Letters.* VIII(6). Mortonhampstead, Devon, U.K.

Matthews, E. R. September, October 1987. Observations on the Portability of Ada I/O. *ACM Ada Letters.* VII(5):100–103.

MacLaren, L. November 1980. Evolving Toward Ada in Real Time Systems. *ACM Sigplan Notices.* 15(11):146–155.

Melliar–Smith, P. M. and B. Randell. March 1987. Software Reliability: The Role of Programmed Exception Handling. *ACM Sigplan Notices.* 12(3):95–100 .

Mowday, B. L. and E. Normand. November 1986. *Ada Programming Standards.* General Dynamics Data Systems Division Departmental Instruction 414.717.

NASA. May 1987. *Ada Style Guide*. Version 1.1, SEL–87–002. Goddard Space Flight Center: Greenbelt, MD 20771.

Nissen, J. C. D., P. Wallis, B. A., Wichmann, et al. 1982. Ada–Europe Guidelines for the Portability of Ada Programs. *ACM Ada Letters*. I(3):44–61.

Nissen, J. and P. Wallis. 1984. *Portability and Style in Ada*. Cambridge University Press.

Pappas, F. March 1985. *Ada Portability Guidelines*. DTIC/NTIS #AD–A160 390.

Pyle, I. C. 1985. *The Ada Programming Language*. second edition. UK:Prentice–Hall International.

Rosen, J. P. November, December 1987. In Defense of the 'Use' Clause. *ACM Ada Letters*. VII(7):77–81.

Ross, D. March–April 1989. The Form of a Passive Iterator. *ACM Ada Letters*. IX(2):102–105.

Rymer, J. and T. McKeever. September 1986. *The FSD Ada Style Guide*. IBM Federal Systems Division Ada Coordinating Group.

Schneiderman, B. 1986. Empirical Studies of Programmers: The Territory, Paths and Destinations. *Empirical Studies of Programmers*. ed. E. Soloway and S. Iyengar. pp. 1–12. Norwood, NJ: Ablex Publishing Corp.

SofTech Inc. December 1985. *ISEC Reusability Guidelines*. Report 3285–4–247/2. also US Army Information Systems Engineering Command. Waltham MA.

Soloway, E., J. Pinto, S. Fertig, S. Letovsky, R. Lampert, D. Littman, K. Ewing. December 1986. Studying Software Documentation From A Cognitive Perspective: A Status Report. *Proceedings of the Eleventh Annual Software Engineering Workshop*. Report SEL–86–006, Software Engineering Laboratory. Greenbelt, Maryland:NASA Goddard Space Flight Center.

Stark M. and E. Seidewitz. March 1987. Towards A General Object–Oriented Ada Lifecycle. In *Proceedings of the Joint Ada Conference*. Fifth National Conference on Ada Technology and Washington Ada Symposium. 213–222.

St.Dennis, R. May 1986. *A Guidebook for Writing Reusable Source Code in Ada* –Version 1.1. Report CSC–86–3:8213. Golden Valley, Minnesota: Honeywell Corporate Systems Development Division.

United Technologies. February 9, 1987. *CENC Programmer's Guide*. Appendix A Ada Programming Standards.

U.S. Department of Defense, Ada Joint Program Office. 1984. *Rationale for the Design of the Ada Programming Language*.

U.S. Department of Defense, Ada Joint Program Office. January 1983. *Reference Manual for the Ada Programming Language*. ANSI/MIL–STD–1815A.

VanNeste, K.F. January/February 1986. Ada Coding Standards and Conventions. *ACM Ada Letters*. VI(1):41–48.

Volz, R. A., Mudge, Naylor and Mayer. May 1985. Some Problems in Distributing Real–time Ada Programs Across Machines. *Ada in Use, Proceedings of the Ada International Conference*. pp. 14–16. Paris.

Index

For convenience, each entry in this index refers to the page number of the beginning of the guideline containing the indexed item rather than the page number on which the indexed item appears.

exception, 120
termination, 86

conditional
    compilation, 172
    entry call, 53, 116, 119, 178
    expression, 26, 83, 139
    statement, 172

configuration control, 45

constant, 32
    as actual parameters to main pro-
        gram, 131
    examples, 187
    expression, 171, 172
    in aggregate initializations, 66, 184
    in establishing interrupt entries, 145
    symbolic, 171

constraint, 34, 70, 100, 135

context
    clause, 15, 48, 51, 92, 94, 178, 182
    compilation, 50, 51, 92
    dependency, 48
    of exceptions, 54
    to shorten names, 28
    unchecked conversion, 100

continuation
    condition, 86
    line, 9, 178

control
    expression, 86
    flow, 96
    nesting, 21, 83, 185
    short circuit, 88, 187
    structure, 9, 21, 95, 178
    synchronization, 110
    thread of, 110

conversion
    exception, 96
    explicit, 72

numeric, 20
type, 70, 81, 100, 137, 148
unchecked, 100

copyright notice, 24, 183

cyclic executive, 120, 142

D

DURATION, 128, 141, 185

dangling references, 76

data
    coupling, 47
    dynamic, 76
    static, 76
    structure, 29, 74, 76, 139, 169, 173

deadlock, 53, 109

declaration
    alignment, 12
    automatic change, 171
    constant, 32
    digits, 135
    exception, 54
    function call in, 103
    grouping, 45
    hiding, 94
    minimization, 48
    name, 55
    named number, 32
    number per line, 15
    numeric, 136
    parameter, 69, 184
    range, 135
    record, 74, 103
    renames, 21, 92, 94
    spacing, 14
    task, 91, 110
    type, 29, 34, 135
    within blocks, 91

F

T

U

unary operator, 8, 177

unchecked conversion, 100, 148

unchecked deallocation, 76, 100, 116, 147

unconstrained array, 72, 139, 172

underscore, 19, 20, 42, 182

unit
 calling, 98
 descriptive comments for, 24
 generic, 66, 158, 166, 170
 library, 42, 45, 48, 51, 92, 103, 120
 program, 14, 30, 45, 51, 102, 133, 178, 182

universal_integer, 32, 128, 185

universal_real, 32, 137

upper case, 20, 21, 182, 183

use clause, 92, 94

user–defined exception, 96, 98

V

variable
 access, 76
 shared, 143

vertical alignment, 8, 11, 12, 181

virtual processor, 110

visibility, 48, 51, 83, 92, 94, 158

W

while loop, 86, 178

with clause, 51, 92